THE FRENCH

JEAN-FRANÇOIS REVEL

The
French

T R A N S L A T E D   B Y   P A U L A   S P U R L I N

GEORGE BRAZILLER, New York

to C.

THE FRENCH

The citizen's first relationship is with his conscience and with morality; let him forget them and he enters into relationship with the law; if he scorns the law, he ceases being a citizen: then begins his relationship with the state power.

—Saint-Just

When one travels in France, one becomes aware of how miraculous it is that there are any Frenchmen who manage to think at all. No nation, it seems to me, has so successfully "exiled" not only the intellectuals inside society, but the whole populace outside culture. But since the entire nation is supposed to participate in this French civilization that flows uninterruptedly from the top to the bottom and back to the top, observers, misled by this naïve notion, pay too little attention to our material poverty, the bleakness of our everyday lives and the ugliness of our homes. There are nations—some with equal and some with even lower standards of living—which would never tolerate these conditions. These are nations which believe as a matter of course that the purpose of work and prosperity is to yield comfort and pleasure above all else. In France, as soon as one leaves certain limited circles—political, literary, sartorial or urban—one does not feel that one is going from the archetype to its imitations, from the origin to the sequel, from the center to the periphery, but that one is plunging into gloom, not seeing culture radiate outward but seeing it disappear. There are indeed centers of creation, but the ideas they generate are neither applied nor imitated outside them, where, in fact, there is only rejection of what these creative centers produce.

There are monuments and parts of our cities whose fame or beauty disguises the fact that in France there are no real cities: that is, urban centers where the most modest house and the most opulent palace are stylistically harmonious. Once you leave these exceptional parts of town, you enter a world where things are not merely plain but hideous . . . where architecture is not just less elegant and monotonously utilitarian but totally nonexistent, where anything goes. Beside the magnificent tenth of our urban area the other nine-tenths is not as the face of a thin man beside that of a well-fed one: it is a bloated mug choked with a four-day growth of beard. Similarly, anyone in France who is familiar with furniture and interior decoration is well aware that taste (even bad taste) in this sphere is limited to only a few thousand Frenchmen. Visit an apartment whose owner is not one of the elite—that is, not one of those few thousand—and you will find not plainness but plain ugliness. French taste is based on prototypes that never go into production.

The same strange schism exists in clothing: France is the country of *couturiers*, the country where the main fashion magazines are published, but it is also the only country where elegance is a sort of profession. If one has neither the time nor the money to practice this profession, one immediately gives up any pretensions to chic. Next to the most elegantly shod feet, one finds nylon socks in sturdy crepe-soled walking shoes. The average Frenchman looks as though he were dressed in his kid brother's shirt, his late uncle's pants and a jacket he picked up from a bench on a subway platform. While economical women's wear has become much better looking in the past ten years (thanks to the scientific divulgations of such magazines as *Elle* and *Marie-Claire*), for men there is no alternative between elegance and shabbiness. And it has nothing to do with money: on weekdays, the clothes of a wealthy retailer or the headmaster of a *lycée* look like those of a convict who, an hour after his release, has just outfitted himself on the cheap at some manufacturer's outlet. Nor is this due to modesty or asceticism but, it seems, to sheer blindness.

A move from one place to another is as much an "exile" as a change in milieu. The concept of Paris versus the provinces is in this respect merely a flattering administrative way of designating a far more radical and ubiquitous phenomenon. The Parisian touch is not necessarily limited to Paris; Frenchmen everywhere—including the Parisians, with the exception of the inhabitants of two or three districts—look like people in a waiting room. Visit a café in any average French city at any hour of the day. You will find men of all ages standing at the bar drinking bad beer or wine; the room is dismal and the furniture uncomfortable, filthy and nondescript. The customers, whose most striking attribute is their supreme self-satisfaction, will be loudly recounting some personal or local mishap or exploit—the tone friendly if the owner is behind the counter, mocking and self-assured when a barmaid is serving. Except for a suggestion of strange and paradoxical phenomena, the tale scarcely goes beyond anything more than the most banal everyday action, such as buying a pack of cigarettes after dinner or putting one's keys on the chest of drawers and not on the table, contrary to a long habit worthy of note. The events of national scope that they discuss are sports, the lottery, cars and television—not the rising cost of living, even in periods when it pinches hardest. One wonders what these Frenchmen have to do with civilization.

Even television, which is supposed to spread culture and information (I'll return to this amusing thesis later on) does not impinge on the Frenchman's consciousness, judging from his conversation, beyond the point that it offers him quiz shows (the most degrading form of amusement) or sports—seen, of course, from a chauvinistic point of view, the only point of view that this least sports-conscious people on earth can understand. As soon as one leaves French cosmopolitan circles and enters a store, home, factory, dance hall or farmhouse, one feels the same oppressive atmosphere of solitude and backwardness, of lives lived far from the mainstream. Beside the flashy enclaves that have sprung up in some cities, where a couple of supermarkets and a few hundred juke boxes have created a poor man's America, there still exists a makeshift twilight zone that is inhabited by newly arrived immigrants. That is what most of our built-up areas look like. (And it is only fair to say that we have many more "built-up areas" than cities.)

You have only to take a good look at Frenchmen as physical specimens, to know where they live, work and relax and what they talk about, to realize that the statistics are quite accurate when they tell us that books—the part of printed matter that is destined for reading in the only real sense of the word—reach something under a million citizens on an occasional basis, and only several tens of thousands regularly. The figures are about the same for daily and weekly papers that sell news, which, though it may be falsified and sensationalist, maintains at least some sort of relation to events on the national and world scene—and is not just limited to sports, horse races, local gossip and the activities of celebrities and royalty.

Thus one begins to understand the political incapacity of the French people. In this area, too, the combination of deception, arrogance and dishonesty (only successful riots can suspend it temporarily) which characterizes the attitude of the "governing bodies" toward the governed, thrusts them apart.

Governing in France means isolation, exclusion, absolute control. The French politician, and even more the French politico, who is a thousand times worse because he is more egoistic and opinionated, never feels that he is the representative of his people but rather that he is their boss. This is why we have never had a single statesman, for the "greatest" have regarded the people only as an instrument on which to strum their narcissistic strains, and never as constituents whose lot they were supposed to improve. This attitude is common to both the civil servant of the lowest echelon and the Head of State: neither considers himself a servant of the people (which he really is) but as the caste superior of the commoner or citizen. The relationship of the Head of State to the citizen is comparable to that of a departmental head to his subordinate. Except for a few brief periods during the French Revolution and the Fourth and Fifth Republics, the French have never elected anyone to power for reasons that had been honestly explained to them, that they could understand, and that had any relationship with what the candidate promised to do, or with the spate of farcical ratiocinations with which he glorified his unauthorized conduct once in the seat of power. A real abyss separates the actions of the rulers from the comprehension of the citizens, and it distinguishes France from all other literate countries with a remotely liberal tradition. It is no mystery, therefore, that France has never had a government that was both impersonal and well organized or that, with exceedingly rare exceptions, state power is wielded alternately by witless windbags and totalitarian tub thumpers.

The French have no head for politics; in this sphere sagacity is not their long suit. No realistic, respectable, equitable and humane political program can hope to hold out for more than a few months, in the French soul, against the alternately scolding and tearful hot air emitted by some nationalistic buffoon. For he is the Frenchman's soulmate: a bemedaled pinhead—liverish, with a lump in his throat and glowering brow—intent on revenge for everything that has been "done" to France and on praise for everything that France has done to others. Well, what has France done—this country that parades and state visits are supposed to "restore" to its former glory (for France is the most "restored" nation in the world)—very well, what has this France done to become so inestimable and irreplaceable? Waged wars. But every country has waged wars. Yes, but none, in the twentieth century, has measured a man's worth exclusively in terms of his military exploits. Germany? But Germany is quite different: it has been subjected to sundry dictatorships and militarist monarchies, but it does not, in time of peace and democracy, obstinately educate its children—through the family, school, official ceremonies and set speeches—to believe that a nation's bloody past constitutes its chief glory. And I really ought to change "chief glory" to "sole glory." First comes the glorification of our battles and banners. Then nothing. Afterward, perhaps a nod to Pasteur and to Cézanne, and a very slight bow to Montaigne—very slight indeed. French literature is used principally as a pleasant topic for ministerial speeches opening foreign trade fairs. What is called "increasing cultural exchanges" means getting bathtubs in exchange for our surplus artichokes, and what is called "extolling the glories of the nation" invariably implies homicide, unless some daring afterthought (bound to be greeted with a certain coldness) suggests the preposterous notion that a few obscure people like "our inventors" (?) or French mothers be included among the "glories of the nation."

The French mania for things military is so great that our political figures habitually bawl out their speeches in "dauntless" martial tones, even when they are merely announcing a new ruling governing the sale of milk. Moreover, the vast majority of our streets and squares—the most colossally spacious, the longest and the widest—bear the names of marshals and battles. While Delacroix is represented only by an alley, Poussin by an impassable street somewhere in Auteuil, Racine and Corneille by two little lanes in Marseille (omitting their native cities, which are obliged to make some sort of observance), the name of Foch and that of a crook like Soult, on the other hand, stretch over thousands of square yards, and there are countless Avenues d'Iéna as well as boulevards named for Gouvion-Saint-Cyr, Suchet and Lannes. Any Frenchman could tell the foreign traveler who asks him for directions: "Just take this street named for the city where my great-grandfather slaughtered your great-grandfather, and you'll soon come to the square which commemorates the extermination of your father by my uncle." In Nantes there is even a school and a statue named for Cambronne. But perhaps Nantes meant to honor the orator and not the soldier, for everyone knows that though the French are more or less indifferent to their writers, they are on the contrary quite willing to believe that their military leaders are masters of the word. Although the Ecole Militaire is not located on the Boulevard Voltaire but, appropriately, on the Place Champ-de-Mars, the Ecole Normale Supérieure is located on the . . . Rue d'Ulm. True, this is perhaps better than calling it the Rue Charles-Péguy or the Rue Teilhard-de-Chardin, which would have branded this dismal street with the same sheeplike mentality that commonly reigns in the Ecole Normale. Ever since Marseille, to its eternal dishonor, named a lycée after Marcel Pagnol, I would just as soon leave the streets to the generals and their blood baths.

My main point, however, is that our official war histories tend to glorify war as war. French tradition never depicts war as an unfortunate expedient to which one must occasionally resort in order to defend a human heritage without which life wouldn't be worth living, but rather as the sum total of national worth. I belong to the generation that was constantly subjected to the story of the Battle of Verdun; and no one ever said that France would have been better off if it hadn't had to fight this battle in order to safeguard its territory. Quite the contrary. Nor was I ever taught, either at home or at school, that it would have been better if national independence had never been threatened and we had thereby been freed of the necessity of fighting the war of 1914–1918. Much less was I taught that this war might have been waged at a smaller cost and with fewer losses if our generals had been less stupid and inhuman. The French subconscious refuses to accept this fact even today, and the silence which greeted the damning revelations in Abel Ferry's *Carnets secrets,* posthumously published in 1954, demonstrates how press and public alike balk at any historical facts that put the war industry and its leaders in a bad light.[1] People don't want to know that the war could have been won with losses of five hundred thousand instead of a million and a half. Besides, most of the glory goes to the leaders, not to these poor dead soldiers (whenever a battle is won, it is always won by a general; whenever a battle is lost, it is always lost by the French people, who "wouldn't fight"); but in any case, the dead are not so much mourned as glorified. The man who falls on the battlefield is never considered an unlucky devil, even if you can prove that his death wouldn't have changed the outcome. America and Britain, with their democratic sensibility, view war as a terrible, painful fact, tolerable only because of its high moral aims. But not France. The war of 1914–1918, with little ideological sense to it, is justified not in terms of the need to protect national independence but as a series of brilliant feats of arms that are praise-

[1] "It is quite disillusioning to note that of the three most important documented studies that came to my attention during the period between the two wars, the first, Norton Cru's book on military manuals, could be published only at the author's expense in an edition limited to a thousand copies and was never reprinted because of a publishers' cabal. The second, Charles Daudet's astonishing *Anthologie du bourrage de crâne* ("Anthology of Eye-wash"), never saw the light of day because his family refused to let it be published. The third, Bellamy's *Vraie et fausse noblesse* ("Real and Fake Nobility"), was also never published." Galtier-Boissières, *Mémoires d'un Parisien,* vol. II.

worthy in themselves. The Second World War has never been represented in France as the war that saved democracy, freedom and human dignity when they were threatened by dictators, racism, slavery and the death of the mind, but only as the war that regalvanized French nationalism; it is interpreted exclusively from a nationalistic point of view. At any rate, that's what the crushing of the Resistance forces inside France by those based in London really means. Putting the emphasis wholly on the struggle for national sovereignty and not on the struggle against Nazism and for civilization reinforced the reactionary leanings of the French subconscious. Moreover, it didn't matter which side won, for each had a military hero on hand to "save France." Triumphant and restored or simply tolerated—in either case France would go on with its parades, medals, *Te Deums*, Unknown Soldiers, moral order and war monuments.

Apropos of war monuments, about ten years ago the weekly paper *Arts* sponsored a contest for photographs of the ugliest examples of state-commissioned art in the country. Naturally, pictures of war monuments poured in, and, again naturally, protests rose on every side. So *Arts* hastened to announce that monuments to the dead of either World War were not eligible. These protestations strike one as passing strange, for raising hideous monuments to the war dead seems to show a deal less respect for France's heroes than the act of pointing out that the monuments themselves are hideous. Furthermore, the commissions for all these monuments went—not without shady behind-the-scenes deals—to artists of indeed monumental mediocrity, and the angry protests came largely from a corrupt gang of local petty officials. As soon as some understrapper blows the whistle, the press is supposed to shut up, even when it supports a cause that is above suspicion. Except for a few suburban Michelangelos, whose creative pride suffered damage, nobody got upset when *Arts* printed hundreds of photographs of awful bas-reliefs adorning schools, post offices and hospitals. The Frenchman's indifference to plastic beauty contrasts strangely with his hyper-sensitivity to anything concerning war cadavers; the glorification of corpses by means of monumental sculptures fills him with an endless paroxysm of pride.

What strikes one most is that this necrophilia is particularly widespread in those professions whose basically civilized nature would lead one to believe that its members would regard the war dead as victims, not heroes; as "losses," not gains. Note, by the way, that the term "losses" designates the dead and wounded only in wartime, never afterward, for during a war a dead man is in fact a "loss" since he hasn't lived to fight another day. Officially, this is the only point of view from which his death should be mourned. After the war, the important thing is to have as many dead as possible, for the greater the number of dead, the greater the glory that accrues to the nation. Members of the above-mentioned "civilized" professions, particularly certain teachers who manage to keep their retroactive bellicosity at a white heat, know this well. I have in mind a director of one of the French Institutes abroad and the headmasters of two lycées where I happened to teach. I never had a conversation with any of these worthies that did not lead to the war of 1914–1918. One—more bloodthirsty than the others—had hung his World War I saber on the wall opposite his desk, and he would refer to himself, with fine periphrasis, as "the owner of that sword." He saw to it that most of the paltry funds earmarked for the library were used to buy works on military history. Another was always available for the chairmanship of veterans' organizations; and peace was tolerable to the third only because he was allowed to organize student parades in front of the war monument in the lycée courtyard on November 11. I spent most of my teaching career under these three men, and never was I able to discuss pedagogical problems with them, let alone literature or philosophy. The only thing that diverted them from their bellicose daydreams would be some banal disciplinary problem, which they always solved with exemplary cowardice if the rebellious student's family happened to have connections. Possibly these three men did have some ideas about their profession, but if so I was unable to discover them. If they had a philosophy of teaching, it remained unfathomable. On the other hand, I knew everything about their strategic theories.

You will argue that this idealization of war, this cult of the soldier—which writers like Norton-Cru, whose books *Témoins* and *Du témoinage* were suppressed by the French subconscious, have analyzed without success—is common to all Indo-European cultures. But aside from Fascist regimes in the highest stage of virulence, in this twentieth century only the successive French republics have glorified the warrior as such. Hence that most curious of French fauna: café proprietors, lycée headmasters, civil engineers, auctioneers and so on who delight in reducing their whole lives to the four or five years that they spent in uniform. They are prouder of being officers on reserve than they are of being civilians on active duty.

This tendency to subordinate to military values all other values is one aspect of the more general state of affairs to which I alluded earlier: the obviously difficult task of getting the French used to thinking democratically, of making democracy an integral part of their tradition. France has had its revolutions, but never has the entire nation lived by the democratic principle of voluntary obedience to the Law, conceived of as the expression of general will. There has always been in France, and today more than ever before, a minority that believes it was born to govern and be the sole fountainhead of sovereignty; in its eyes the institutions of the state—molded or modified by popular pressure and hence usurpations—have always counted for nought. One is struck by how scrupulously the French support "republican legality" in times when there are no storms on the political horizon; by the way they insist on calling themselves "good republicans" in the very periods (if there have been any) when a *coup d'état* seems least likely; by the expression of concern on their faces when they wonder whether such and such a general possesses "republican sentiments."

I remember vividly the occasion in 1949 when the Cultural Relations Office assigned me to fill a teaching position in Mexico and I had to be vetted by the omnipotent Dr. Paul Rivet, then director of the Musée de l'Homme. The visit had been arranged by the office that had appointed me, for no assignment to Mexico could be filled without Dr. Rivet's blessing—an instance of that characteristic practice in French public life, whereby the influence of the individual far surpasses the limits of his office. At any rate, I was subjected to an hour-long monologue by this illustrious ethnologist, and, needless to say, it was of absolutely no scientific value. During this time I could escape staring neither at his three-dimensional photograph (the specialty of a gag and gimmick emporium at the upper end of the Champs-Elysées), nor at his bust mounted behind him on a sort of pedestal or bookshelf (for with the French idea of power goes a strong tendency to narcissism, and intellectual leaders are no less prone to it than others); and, listening to Dr. Rivet's observations, I was surprised by what he said of our then ambassador to Mexico: "I believe him to be a sincere republican." The need to mention such a detail in 1949 struck me as exceedingly droll, for I was naïve enough to believe that after Nazism and Pétain's National Revolution people could be more or less progressive, but that no one could possibly be anti-republican.

However, the following decade showed that Dr. Rivet had not uttered empty words, for we saw universal suffrage travestied by the election law of 1951,[2] deputies lending their support to policies contrary to those for which they had been elected, and state funds going to subsidize religious schools; we saw falsification of news grow to ever larger proportions, the suppression of civil liberties become increasingly common, and laws designed to protect the citizen fall into desuetude. There followed a series of *coups d'état*—some successful, some not— which filled the constitutional vacuum and made it possible to abolish the very principle of the separation of powers. But the tedious story of our political decline is too well known to merit further elaboration. Moreover, my point at the moment is merely to emphasize how ready the Frenchman is to relinquish legal ownership of his patch of land if only someone will kindly allow him to cultivate it. This is why support of "republican legality" is really the counter-current in French politics. Even when in power our republicans have always opposed that "profound legitimacy" of which de Gaulle does well to speak, since this is what has always conferred *a priori* legitimacy on our governing class of generals, bishops, business heads, high officials and financiers who, except for a few rare exceptions, have and still maintain themselves in power by mutually electing and re-electing one another to office. Notwithstanding their violent revolutions, the French venerate nobility. In their eyes "legitimacy" and legality are a twain that rarely meet. In 1958, at the time of the de Gaulle putsch, the Leftists were exchanging "republican greetings" and the extreme Rightists "nationalist greetings." We are not only used to considering the concepts "republic" and "nation" as

[2] The law was extremely complicated but its main provision was the system of *apparentements*, which operated as follows: in given constituencies certain parties could be "associated" (*apparentées*) and put up a single ticket which all the associated parties would support. If the ticket polled more than half the vote, the associated parties would take all the seats of the constituency. The seats would then be apportioned among the parties making up the pool, roughly according to their share of the popular vote. The effect of the law was to penalize parties that put up single tickets, *i.e.*, the Communist party in particular.—*Translator's note.*

13

antithetical, but we consider respect for law to have nothing to do with either. Can you imagine two Americans or two Britons exchanging "constitutional" or "legally valid" greetings? That you cannot is because they do not lie under a political system in which one easily passes from verbal disagreement to illegal acts and equally easily, when the occasion demands, from the possession of power to the abolition of civil liberties.

Since the reign of Law never really became established in France, it is natural that the reign of individuals—of those who are traditionally on the strongest side—should be accepted by a people which, except during riots and rebellions, is more inclined than any other to respect false dignity—and today more easily than ever, because for twenty years it has been the most ill-informed people on earth. One small detail shows how much less prestige we attach to political power when it derives from the people than when it is seized by a strong man, when it originates in the collectivity than when it is based on a personality, when the leader considers himself the representative of his fellow citizens and one who can be removed from office, than when he sets himself up above them in the name of that small influential group that constitutes "legitimate power." That little detail is simply that in France when a general becomes President of the Republic he is called "General" more often than "President." The title of President of the Republic—which is to say that the man incarnates the public interest, represents the entire nation—is undoubtedly more imposing than the word designating a high military officer. But not in France—a nation whose ruling class has never favored republican ideals, representative government or political power conceived of as temporarily held in trust.

After Eisenhower became President, he was never referred to as "General," and he never wore his uniform; for eight years he was "Mr. President." When Marshall was appointed Secretary of State by Truman, he automatically ceased being considered a general as long as he held this office. On the other hand, in France as in Mexico, a general-president remains primarily a general, or, better, he is a kind of quick-change artist who dons first civil and then military attire as circumstances and audience seem to demand. We French can be thankful that our General's generalship was not of the cloth, for a chaplain-general would have offered a third sartorial possibility to our bedazzled eyes. The idea of suiting one's costumes to the content of one's speeches ought, perhaps, to be maintained. Our civilian presidents were so colorless that we needed a revival of baroque opulence and natural variety. Indeed, the practice should be extended: we would see the Chief of State dressed in a gardener's apron to open flower shows, in mechanic's overalls to open the Automobile Show— just as we saw him in miner's get-up when he addressed the crowds at Pas-de-Calais.

The psychological make-up of the French often favors self-arrogated power, and France always has a couple of saviors in reserve (something that you would never find in England) who are not only ready to seize power in time of crisis but who will even hasten on the crises themselves. The people regard candidates who solicit votes as "dopes" and politics as a mug's game; and yet the candidate is only an ordinary citizen who addresses himself to his fellow citizens as an equal —which is or ought to be more praiseworthy than the political swindles of a Louis Napoléon or a Pétain, who, though now reviled, were wholeheartedly venerated by their contemporaries. From Maurice Barrès to the *Gringoire*,[3] from Charles Maurras to Michel Debré, from Pétain's National Revolution

[3] Owned by the millionaire Horace de Carbuccia, *Gringoire* was violently anti-parliamentary and anti-British, pro-Nazi and pro-Fascist. In the late thirties its circulation reached 700,000 and its influence was felt throughout France. It is credited with having hounded Roger Salengro, Minister of the Interior under Léon Blum, to suicide and with having created the military defeatism that led to the fall of France in June, 1940.—*Translator's note.*

to the "Renovation," the people have always reacted to the denigration of parliamentarism with much more enthusiasm than the defects of that system seem to warrant. In the greatest anti-parliamentary pamphlet ever written, *Leurs Figures*, Maurice Barrès attempted to destroy representative government but unwittingly put his finger on its strong point. In his detailed account of the development of the Panama scandal, he keeps repeating that you cannot have parliamentary government without corruption. But the facts he cites demonstrate that without Parliament the scandal would never have been uncovered.

A paradox the Right has never ceased exploiting during the course of our history has it that democracy provides the conditions to overthrow democracy. We may take the ever-increasing acceptance of this sophism as the true measure of French intelligence. Obviously, anyone who has power to dispense is ready prey to corrupting influences, and under the parliamentary system deputies are open game. Nevertheless, bribery is more difficult to hush up when you have a parliament. Indeed, this is one of the reasons why the institution came into being. But under authoritarian regimes deals between politicians and businessmen are hatched out of the public eye—there being no body with investigatory powers and no power other than The Power—and consequently the Frenchman considers such regimes to be "cleaner" than parliamentary ones. Moreover, respect for power is so great in France that the muckraker is considered more reprehensible than the muck he rakes. Or, to be more exact, the public accepts the slanders dreamed up by the Fascist right against a Léon Blum, a Jean Zay, a Roger Salengro, a Georges Mandel,[4] a Pierre Mendès-France or a François Mitterrand, but greets

[4] Jean Zay and Georges Mandel were ministers in Paul Reynaud's government in the spring of 1940. They were later murdered by Darnand's pro-Nazi militia.—*Translator's note.*

charges of torture in Algeria or piaster trafficking in Indochina with skepticism. The Frenchman is only too happy to believe any tale about the crookedness of Left-wing politicians, but he will never quite accept proof of chicanery or lack of patriotism on the part of the Right. The charge of collaboration with the Nazi Occupation was not by itself strong enough to impugn the patriotism of Vichyites, even when they accumulated fortunes through their collaboration. "The worst of Chambers is better than the best of antechambers," said Cavour—a statement no Frenchman would believe. Antechambers fill him with awe. He would rather have the windy, condescending press handouts of a minister of information than the report of a legislator elected by the people, the patronizing and incomprehensible lectures of some lawyer than the explanation of his elected representative in accordance with the duties of his trust.

When a nation stops thinking, unanimity reigns. The conservatives argue that politics divide the French. The argument carries weight only if one forgets that diversity of opinion is normal and healthy in a democracy where the dissenters subsequently bow to majority rule. To force unity on the nation by making dissent practically impossible and all but illegal pushes the problem to one side but does not solve it. Democracy is a way of resolving disagreement. But the French have been led to believe that it is politically salubrious to make sure that disagreement does not exist. They fall into this obvious trap periodically. Another traditional anti-parliamentary view is the stubborn illusion that the turmoil of representative government keeps the executive power from functioning smoothly. Thanks to the intellectual sleight of hand of the Rightists, the French tend to confuse the *technical* problem of establishing an efficient executive power with the *de principe* problem regarding the source of sovereignty. Whether or not the man and party whom the majority elects to the executive power (assuming that the elections are truly democratic) will subsequently be able really to exercise this power is an organizational problem of the same kind that exists in the United States, and it does not at all imply that the power should derive from any other source than an honestly informed and enlightened electorate. But in this as in nearly every other area, the average Frenchman's regard for military authority distorts his concept of public life, making it impossible for him to conceive of a purely civilian state power emanating from adults with an average intellectual endowment.

To gauge the degree to which the military image dominates French life, one need only consider the kind of writer whose popularity spreads beyond both the literary world and the reading portion of the bourgeoisie to influence, directly or indirectly, the entire population. The most successful of these writers in the last thirty years is Saint-Exupéry, the flyboy who replaced the human brain with an airplane engine. All his propeller-driven yarns spin endless hosannahs to the *chef* (a word which, when used without a complement, should be reserved for master cooks) and to the ably commanded and disciplined "team." Saint-Exupéry, who is a favorite subject of the gentlemen who compose the Bachot exams and who has inundated railway newsstands, paperback and de-luxe editions, literary reviews and weeklies (and it takes a lot of ingenuity to rehash so thin a subject matter in one special number after another) . . . Saint-Exupéry has become more than a writer: he is a saint and a prophet. To understand France, one has to realize that its most influential writer is not Gide or Breton but Saint-Ex, who taught the French that prolix idiocies become profound philosophic truths at an altitude of seven thousand feet. Put stupidity in a cockpit and it looks like wisdom, and our young people have eagerly lapped it up. I remember how important André Maurois's *Dialogues sur le Commandement* was considered back in 1935. It was enormously popular among the middle class during the thirties: teachers discussed it in class, and the veteran read it of an evening, one hand resting on his helmet and the other holding his glass of brandy. The appalling stupidity of these dialogues made the book a bestseller, and the key to its success lay in the fact that Maurois sought to justify, in apparently reasonable tones, the "mystique of the Leader." Like any good salesman, all he did was give the public what it wanted. He aimed to demolish Jean de Pierrefeu's troubling *Plutarque a menti*, which exploded the legends that propaganda had woven around the principal agents of the slaughter of 1914–1918. Maurois based his argument not on facts but on mere declarations of principle and salvaged the legends of these military leaders, including (by the bye) Marshal Pétain. Supporting Bergson, whose *Deux Sources*, written during the same period, also glorified the "hero," Maurois writes: "It was not the Roman army but Caesar that conquered Gaul." Likewise, a few years later the French were to say: "We are not occupied by the enemy; we are governed by the Marshal." And again: "The liberation of France was accomplished not by the Allied forces or by the Resistance movement but by General de Gaulle single-handed." The ease with which a leader—and he need not even have a program—can gain power in France by referendum or merely by acclamation proclaims France's kinship with the Latin countries and with Latin America in particular. In order to succeed in such countries a statesman must primarily be a celebrity—a state of affairs that indicates a pretty low level of political sophistication. It remains only to explain how a people with the reputation of having a great revolutionary tradition manages to get along most of the time quite comfortably at precisely this level.

Revolutionary tradition aside, our people in some obscure fashion identify authority, efficiency, military command, stability, glory and a strong army, as evidenced by the enthusiasm with which, at the height of the hedonistic vacation exodus, they greeted the military parade in Paris on July 14, 1964. Carried away by their junior-size *force de frappe* and their rifles of a different calibre from those of the other NATO countries, French youth shows itself still true to the spirit of the Marne. When one sees the President of the Fifth "Republic" on an official visit to Italy eagerly don his uniform to visit Solferino and extol—to the huge delight of the public —one of the goriest bloodbaths of the nineteenth century; when one sees that books which avowedly aim to "wake France up" appeal (and very successfully) to chauvinism, militarism, anti-intellectualism and anti-democratic ideals (Jean Dutourd's *Les Taxis de la Marne* and Michel Debré's *Ces Princes qui nous gouvernent*); when one sees our policemen intent on protecting the government instead of the citizens; when one sees persecution tolerated provided that it is well-established, helmeted, consecrated and respectable and its methods of oppression subtle and omnipresent; and when, on the other hand, one sees authority threatened, discredited, scorned and vituperated whenever it emanates from the people, one. is led to believe that French letters and the French revolutionary tradition must be fundamentally at odds with the French themselves. One begins to realize that liberty, thought and revolutionary ideals are not the products of French society but rather its antithesis, and that they have never figured in its collective life and thought with any degree of durability.

We French are fond of citing that famous apostrophe of "a great friend of France" (doubtless in the pay of the Quai d'Orsay): "O France, second homeland of all well-born men!" How many Frenchmen are worthy of having this "for export only" France, in which intelligence and freedom supposedly reign, for a second homeland?

*

The foregoing pages may sound as though my main objective is to criticize the Fifth Republic. But that is not my intent. In the first place, the Fifth Republic has already been subjected to criticism from a democratic point of view. There have been studies of its laws and institutions that show how, rapidly but imperceptibly, the Fifth Republic destroyed the legal infrastructure that France had evolved since the Revolution, and abolished the balance and separation of powers, the principle of representative government, freedom of public media, the popular basis of justice, the individual's guarantees against abuses of power and his means of protection against the encroachments of the State.[5] Consequently, it would be pointless to go on in the same vein, particularly since the French today cannot be moved by argument. Our grandchildren will one day learn how passive we were, and they will be astonished at how our elite persisted in denying the obvious. Moreover, I should like to point out that I am less concerned with the Fifth Republic in itself than I am with the way it embodies certain profound tendencies of the French psyche. While the Fifth Republic unquestionably represents a break in the continuity of our institutions, it seems to me that it completely fulfills our moral aspirations. If I mention things and events from its seven-year history, it will not be because of their political significance, but because they reveal something salient in the psychology of my compatriots.

General de Gaulle is quite right when he thinks that he symbolizes France; but he is wrong to consider this the least bit flattering. For the symbol and the symbolized make a sorry pair, and each only emphasizes the faults of the other. So long as parliamentary institutions separated them, both the "real France" and de Gaulle were uncertain that they were on the right path, but once rid of those bothersome Communists who

[5] See in particular François Mitterrand, *Le Coup d'Etat permanent*, Paris, 1964.

had stymied them in 1944, they entered into a fruitful partnership in 1958.

Consequently, many Frenchmen and friends of France are prone to think that all those regimes—authoritarian, paternalistic, monarchist, Catholic, imperialistic, dictatorial, militaristic, provisional and emergency, and regimes of moral order, of strengthening, of renovation, of union, of rally and of restoration—which dot our history since 1789, are merely wanderings off the straight democratic, revolutionary path. But this is by no means the case. This type of regime is the norm in France; what are exceptional are governments inspired by the people. In all, they span about four years at the end of the eighteenth century, a few months in 1848, a total of about four years scattered throughout the Third Republic and two or three months after the Liberation. Moreover, the majority of the reforms that were instituted during these brief intervals have been destroyed by clever, hypocritical maneuvering. And what has survived is negligible compared to the heritage of authoritarian regimes. We have retained about as many—if not more—of the laws and administrative and police procedures of the Vichy regime as we have of the laws of the Popular Front and of the infant Fourth Republic. True, the Third Republic often gave France Rightist governments, but although they were socially reactionary, they at least respected the constitution, which is better than deceitful demagogy with no constitution. But important segments of the public have always refused to acknowledge the legality of republican government. That is why it is only too easy these days to condemn, in the name of a hodgepodge of technocracy and Marxism, the "old-fashioned liberalism" of the very political figures to whom we owe our laws on the freedom of the press, public education, the separation of Church and State and the freedom of political dissent. And yet such laws *are* outdated at the moment, but only in the sense that if today in 1965 we tried to apply them as honestly and literally as they were applied in the past it would be tantamount to a violent revolution. Admittedly liberalism is subject to attack—but not under an authoritarian regime. Admittedly parliamentarism can be criticized—but not in the name of nepotism and the spoils system. Admittedly "catering to the vote" can be ridiculed—but not in the name of catering to personal interests. But where is all this censure, scorn and ridicule coming from?[6]

It is quite easy to see how the slow task of undermining democratic institutions, so doggedly pursued by the Right since 1875, has finally left its mark on public opinion. In fact, as I have already said, France entertains democratic illusions only on paper and in history texts. To the average Frenchman this history is only a kaleidoscope of regimes and has nothing to do with his daily life, particularly since he has stopped "being interested in politics" once and for all. The usual sort of political education in France, first undertaken by the schools at the end of the nineteenth century, only to be immediately quashed by boos and catcalls, stops considerably short of Montesquieu. The most widespread concept of power in France is that of the leader, the "boss," to whom one may "appeal" for some favor (with varying degrees of success, depending on his humor), but as a rule such appeals are frowned on, for our duty is to "help" him and not to "annoy" him. This is why militant activities and simple criticism alike on the part of the Left are always severely condemned; indeed, these activities—particularly strikes—engender strong guilt feelings within the Left itself, for they "annoy" the leader just when he is stabilizing the franc, "building up" the nation and making France "strong" and "respected abroad." Therefore,

[6] After the municipal elections of March, 1965, which dampened the hopes of the official party, certain Leftist commentators intrepidly demanded the resignation of the premier, who they claimed had been morally defeated. And these were the men who had long insisted that the principle of representative government was outmoded!

23

this is "not the right time" for personal opinions. The French have never understood that once the "right time" is passed, they face an accomplished fact, and their freely but retrospectively expressed opinion has only an historical interest. And this is due to the fact that to date they have never realized that the source of power rests within themselves, not outside.

It was, therefore, inevitable that the Right would one day succeed in setting up an a-constitutional government that would continue to "build up" the nation—permanently and forcibly. And the prosperity that Europe has enjoyed since 1950 made it even easier to perpetuate this form of government. Once Frenchmen—always in the vanguard of moral and intellectual progress, tireless artificers of subcultural propaganda—once, I repeat, these Frenchmen had got over their bothersome scruples about a conservative and nationalist regime (for the last one had been allied with the Nazis during the terrors of the Occupation), they gave the world a glimpse of an unprecedented political phenomenon: *a dictatorship in a period of prosperity*—whose first effect was to curtail prosperity.

It is understandable that, after the long period of poverty and crisis that the French had to endure up to 1950, most Frenchmen should have abandoned themselves to the bliss of working almost regularly, eating almost enough to satisfy their hunger, almost discovering what leisure time is, and so put up with being poorly housed and poorly educated because instead of these things they have television sets and cars (or at least the possibility of owning a car). And all this becomes even more understandable when we look at it from another angle: we are dealing with a people that has had propaganda for authoritarian systems hammered into it throughout its history. And so the French believe that good things are blessings bestowed on them by the government, not the just fruits of their labors. I find nothing surprising in the present situation, which in my opinion is in keeping with French psychology. I cannot repeat often enough that we must get over the notion that France is a fundamentally democratic country. During my lifetime I have seen two authoritarian governments enjoy extraordinary popularity, even when everything was going badly. I have also seen two democratic governments encounter extraordinary unpopularity, even when things on the whole were going quite respectably. Therefore I've given up believing that the French are capable either of adopting a political program because they understand it, or of judging its effectiveness once it has been applied. Prosperity permits people to indulge their whims: the French have treated themselves to a dictatorship. They are paying dearly, but they do so gladly, just as they prefer having an automobile to having decent housing.

On the present political scene, however, there is a new phenomenon: the disappearance of any real opposition from the intellectuals. There is a lot of talk about the vanishing Left. For the Left to obtain enough votes to come to power in France—or to take part in the government—requires a concurrence of circumstances that takes place about as often as the return of Halley's comet. On the other hand, what is always possible, what has no reason to surrender even in the face of concrete misfortunes, is ideological opposition. Much of French thought has consisted in "think against" because there has very rarely been anything in France to "think for." This has given rise to the split between our culture and our everyday life, which seems to me to be a constant factor in our history.

I am not maintaining that all French culture leans left and all French life leans right, even though the formula seems to hold in the long view. The very number and marked influence of Rightist thinkers in our own century (to say nothing of the devastation wrought by reactionary ideas masquerading as progressive thought) make it impossible to maintain that French intellectual life and the struggle for human rights are synonymous. The Vichy regime had no trouble finding apologists to justify it and poets to sing its praises.[7] But if we look at our history since 1944, we can say without exaggeration that our dominant philosophic and literary currents—dominant both in quantity and in quality—tend to the Left. For this reason it is well worth looking into the question of why the intellectual Left has vanished over the past twenty years—or at any rate has fallen short even of espousing the causes of its favorite butt, old-fashioned liberalism—why it puts up such a weak defense of its ideology, and why, in any event, it has ceased to have the slightest influence on the course of events and on public opinion.

There are various explanations for the decline. The first can be traced to the lack of doctrinal unity that characterized the Left intelligentsia from the start: after the war the general feeling was pro-Left, but the reasons for an individual's taking a revolutionary stand were many and varied. Thus, the union of such strange bedfellows, grounded as it was on an ideologi-

[7] I take a random example which I clipped from the sales catalogue of a bookshop. Excerpt from a handwritten letter from Paul Léautaud to Fritz Vanderpyl (1942): ". . . Your brochure on Jewish painting delighted me—even though Valéry once told me that I talk about painting like a man of letters, that is to say, as though I didn't know what I was talking about. For twenty years or more I have never ceased being appalled at the ugliness of contemporary painting. When Apollinaire published *Alcools* with his portrait by Picasso . . . there was certainly something Jewish about Apollinaire: his bohemian turn of mind, his erudite tales reminiscent of those of Marcel Schwob, the way he has of putting together unrelated bits in his poems ("La chanson du Mal-Aimé"); I remember telling him that it was like a street urinal that you keep walking around and around but can't find the entrance to. How many times have I stopped to look at the masterpieces of some of the painters that you mention, the phenomenal Chagall among others, wondering what sort of mind, what vision or what formidable (?) you'd have to have to produce such things." Here in the words of that truly French individualist Léautaud we find the perfect expression of the Nazi theory of contemporary art: Jewish and degenerate.

cal muddle, could only prove their weakness, not their strength. Many Leftist intellectuals were Communists; others were Marxists but not "card-carrying members" of the party; still others were existentialists and Christian personalists. Bourgeois society, not understanding the reasons for the quarrels that arose among these various groups, considered them *en masse* as inimical to their own values. While this was not untrue, what the middle class failed to realize was that on certain important points these various Leftist groups were as seriously opposed to one another as they were to the bourgeoisie and that, conversely, on other important points they were in agreement with the bourgeoisie and not with their fellow Leftists.

The only way the opposition of the Left could hope to remain united was by opposing nothing. Thus, the Communists supported historical and dialectic materialism and sought economic revolution, but remained petit-bourgeois in their moral attitudes, academics in art and literature and opportunists in religious matters. Their conformist attitude culminated in their refusal to take the side of revolution during the Algerian War; they unearthed Leninist pamphlets which proved that a Communist soldier's first duty is to slaughter and torture for the reaction; and they left the young so-called Communists without the slightest advice as to what course they should take in this war of oppression. The existentialists, for their part, exerted a liberating influence in the moral sphere, thanks to the shock value of notions like authenticity, liberty, engagement, responsibility, existential aim, ambiguity, etc. But only a fraction of the initiates who bandied such terms about had any idea of their philosophic meaning. For the most part, existentialism provided a climate in which a few slogans could be aired, not a system of thought. It was classified as Leftist primarily because its exponents individually happened to be Leftists. From an ideological point of view, it was generally considered reactionary—particularly by Marxists and psychoanalysts—because it affirmed that consciousness constituted absolute "liberty" and was not dependent on sociological and psycho-physiological conditions. Its anti-rationalism and its patronizing attitude toward science were also thought of as reactionary. Naturally, I am referring to the first stage of existentialism, the stage which characterized the period, not the updating that Sartre attempted fifteen years later in *The Critique of Dialectic Reason*, where he tried to add a little historical determinism to his self-service doctrine of freedom through consciousness. As for the Christian Left, what it gave to the middle class with one hand it took back with the other and, by disrupting the traditionally anti-clerical united front of the revolutionary opposition, it paid orthodoxy in an updated faith for what it demanded of the bourgeoisie in social justice. The only trouble was that orthodoxy was much quicker to welcome their faith than it was to satisfy their demands for justice.

In short, the Leftist intellectual coalition lacked ideological unity. I speak, of course, of intellectuals as such, that is, writers capable of influencing politics through their thought and writing, not through direct action. I want to make this clear, because Leftist intellectuals have all too often mistaken themselves for a political party. In a party, theoretical differences must often be sacrificed in the interest of unity of action. Now, unity of action is desirable only if one is devoted to action and not to thought. While it can be advantageous to sacrifice one's personal views in the case of elections, it is harmful when one is collecting a couple of dozen signatures at the bottom of a petition. If your role is to think and write, your most effective weapon is thought and the printed word, not numbers. The Left did not see fit to elaborate a complete system of revolutionary thought, with a view to strengthening and unifying their philosophic, scientific, moral, political, economic and religious positions, and this defeated them from the start. And after this preliminary defeat, all their other battles, no matter how noble their cause, amounted to nothing more than so many insect bites.

What, indeed, could the reaction possibly have to fear from such a divided opposition? The Communists went on cautiously advocating a few economic reforms, but in the moral sphere they supported the bourgeois family virtues, just as the established authorities did. The existentialists, because of their notions of engagement and responsibility, needed to feel solidarity with the persecuted, both at home and abroad, but their anti-determinist and anti-rationalist doctrine undermined the very foundations of revolutionary thought and so prepared their public to join in the crusades of the magicians, mystics and mystifiers;[8] and the left-wing Christians completed the job of divorcing political action from its philosophic bases.

In sum, the French intellectuals gave the reactionaries real grounds for rejoicing: from the Communists they received a conformist, family-based morality; from the existentialists the most attractive and influential anti-rationalist doctrine since Bergson; and from the left-wing Christians a new, more tempting version of Christianity. And so Fascist thought tempered its sword in the river of the Left, and each current helped in some way to strengthen it. The points on which the intellectuals remained in agreement—for social justice, against racism, for the colonized peoples and, later, against the nuclear deterrent—made not the slightest impression on those in power, for each of the three having been beaten on separate issues, they were defeated as a body, since their weaknesses, not their strengths, were complementary.

Hence, with each passing year, their intervention grew

[8] The reference here is to the phenomenally successful *The Morning of the Magicians* by Louis Pauwels and Jacques Bergier and to the equally successful magazine that Pauwels edits, *Planète*. Both the book and the magazine explore the relationship of occult phenomena to science. ESP, acupuncture, alchemy, Teilhard de Chardin—such are Pauwels favorite subjects, and thanks to his magazine they are now familiar to the average Frenchman.—*Translator's note.*

progressively less effective. Where Voltaire, Hugo and Zola succeeded thanks to the justness and accuracy of their aim (in keeping with the justness and accuracy of their general positions), the postwar French intellectuals were taken about as seriously as if they were fifty small businessmen, hairdressers and plumbers agitating for a Ph. D. reform. Their petitions in favor of the persecuted, the accused, the condemned to death and those who had disappeared without trace, which used to appear regularly in the newspapers above more or less the same signatures, usually merely precipitated what they were intended to prevent. None of the torturers whom the left-wing intellectuals demanded be brought to justice were ever summoned before the judge. Indeed, almost as though in defiance of them, the rights of man have been flagrantly violated even when politics was not at issue, until now such violations are common practice. In France today, innocent witnesses or citizens who have been dragged off to the police station by mistake may be clubbed to death, and the policemen who committed the crime summarily acquitted by the court—if, indeed, they are even charged. On the other hand, a citizen who *accidentally* kills a policeman will unfailingly be sentenced to death, and the protests of our most distinguished writers fall on deaf ears, for they do not have the slightest effect on either the government or public opinion. Contrary to one of the many complacent myths that we have created about ourselves, France is no longer a nation in which the intellectuals play any part in public affairs or have any influence on the thought of the masses.

But there is another more recent and more comprehensible reason for the impotence of the intelligentsia: namely, that most French intellectuals have ceased opposing the government, even *platonically*. At first, the intellectual opposition was merely ineffectual. Now, it has ceased to exist, having lost the desire to exist.

Let us trace the evolution that has taken place in an intellectual who was twenty years old between 1945 and 1955. First we see him as a Communist whose good or bad relations with the party depend on the degree to which he is attracted to or repelled by Stalinism; in 1956, after the Hungarian uprising was crushed by Soviet troops, we find him either a Communist "of the opposition" (ready to engage in a much more wearisome and futile struggle with the leadership of the party than that waged by the whole of the proletarian forces against capitalism since the beginning of capitalist society) or, having left the Communist party, helping to found one or several of the Leftist splinter parties that flourished between 1956 and 1962—groups in which you always found the same large number of familiar faces and the same tiny core of real militants. At the time of the de Gaulle putsch of May, 1958, we naturally find our man a vigilant republican; he hurries to the Place de la Nation, where he joins the parade of three or four hundred thousand other Parisians and reaches the Place de la République at the precise moment when the institution for which it was named passes into oblivion. After that, he takes part—courageously, for the Gaullist police are tough customers—in the various street demonstrations for peace in Algeria and against torture. In 1961, however, we find him a somewhat sheepish Gaullist, and in 1962 an all-out Gaullist—or at least, in order not to seem a turncoat, he has all the earmarks of the Gaullist except for the name and official membership in the party.

This evolution could be quite honorably justified if it were a calculated one and based on considerations of *Real politik*. But we may be pardoned a certain curiosity and suspicion when it is characterized by the vehemence of an unreasoning emotional conversion (camouflaged by contradictory explanations) of men whom all objections leave merely irritated or indifferent. Although such passivity is natural and quite expected from most of the French electorate, it is surprising when it occurs in cultivated people whose thought and very existence seemed to be nourished by an encyclopedic political formation. We are therefore somewhat astonished to see them so bamboozled by a rather rudimentary propaganda campaign that they are willing to make the supreme sacrifice of renouncing their right to think.

The conversion to Gaullism through this sacrifice was completed in the streets in 1962, when the Fifth Republic repressed the Leftist demonstrators (eight were clubbed to death) who were protesting against . . . the crimes of the anti-Gaullist right-wing extremists! Such sacrifice in the realm of political doctrine is no less zealous and is even more sophisticated than it is in political action, for the government does not even have to crack any skulls, and it takes place in a closed circuit. Why should the government bother to maintain an official censorship when its presumptive adversaries convert themselves independently and so much more cheaply? What characterizes our dictatorship is not so much that it has all the means it needs to suppress its enemies (who have few or no constitutional weapons to protect themselves) but that it hardly ever needs to resort to repression. It is, partly, a dictatorship in essence but not in fact—a state of affairs that enables it to deny that it is a dictatorship at all. Self-censorship supplants active repression. Our intellectuals are bathed in submissiveness, as their predecessors were consumed by intransigence. By and large they are happy to enjoy toleration—not to exercise a right—provided, of course, that they are allowed to print an occasional respectful demurrer and can permit themselves to be titillated by the latest disrespectful caricature. "How free we are in France!" they chortle every week when Le Canard enchaîné appears, so strange it seems to them to be free at all. Except in periods of famine, do we yelp with joy when we find bread and salt on the table? And in order for the government to go on suppressing freedom of opinion, thought and expression, opinion, thought and expression have to exist.

Do not think that absent-mindedness or solely the heat of passion leads me into taking up the same idea again and again. We French are fond of saying that it is the art of understatement that characterizes the good taste of the French. But in fact what is merely suggested, hinted at, is in grave danger of going unheeded in this country where, in both politics and culture, everything is based on propaganda, that is, on repetition. It would be foolhardy to assume that a French reader can absorb more than one argument at a time; in order to penetrate the threshold of his consciousness, one must repeat and repeat and repeat.

As I was saying, it is essential to a nation's tranquillity and to the even tenor of its ways—including those of its thinkers and writers—for governments to be constantly and unfailingly reminded of what they are: namely, servants of the people and not heaven-sent philanthropists. Notwithstanding certain injustices and hypocrisy that have characterized parliamentary governments in the past, dictatorships and representative governments are worlds apart: on the one hand we have nations which no longer even question the principle that power derives from the Law and the Law from the people, and on the other nations where power is tainted with unhealthy effluvia and the putrefactions emanating from the ancient image of a superhuman war chief and of a high priest endowed with sacred powers. Whatever the faults and limitations of parliamentarism, the proper way to correct them is not to undermine the basic principle of the source of power, but to reform the *technical* workings of the institution. Let the means whereby the people's will is expressed, and the executive power held in check, be what they will—so long as they exist. Not all our oligarchs, nor all their hectoring allusions to the vast complexities of their plans (on which the bureaucracies of state and monopoly collaborate, and which they wouldn't hesitate to reveal if they were really so hard to understand) will ever convince me otherwise. It is this type of power, in which state secrets and blackmail flourish side by side, that puts France—where democracy, I repeat, has always been the counter-current—among the politically archaic, pre-juridical civilizations; and, again I repeat, I do not regard the Fifth Republic as atypical of us French but, on the contrary, as a faithful reflection of our deepest desires. Now that a united Europe is on the horizon—despite fuss and despite us—it would perhaps be well if the other nations of Europe got it clear that the democratic principle has never been firmly rooted in France, and that it seems unlikely that it will take hold in the near future.

Now, the very fact that the Frenchman considers that his leaders possess by inheritance the power that they wield gives rise to distorted judgments when he comes to evaluate the way in which the power is exercised. Such distortions are evident especially among intellectuals and, recently, among intellectuals of the Left. They derive from one simple formula, the automatic application of which accomplishes a miracle of propaganda. Simply stated, under a democratic regime, all the good a government does is taken for granted, for it has merely done its duty; hence, no one would dream of being grateful. What really counts are the things it does badly, for that is generally all that anyone remembers. This is why the plus side of the history of democracies remains anonymous, while the minus side is associated with loathed figures. Under the archaic regime, on the other hand, the bad things are attributed to insurmountable difficulties ("no one else could have done any better"—no proof required) or to the incompetence of the preceding government (even if it fell from power at the time of the first sputniks) if not to world hostility (an elevated xenophobia oils the gears of personal power). And all good

34

things, including the vernal equinox, are attributed to the personal action of the Chief of State and his team. With dictatorships, it is the bad side of their histories that is always anonymous and the good that is always associated with some figure (and with several incidental figures).

What's new about this miracle, however, is the enthusiasm with which the intellectuals of the opposition have pounced on the formula. They have proceeded to apply it so frenetically that it has yielded more than the government ever dreamed.

I will forgo a detailed analysis of the way the Left has employed this formula, for the intricacies thereof would demand perilous mental exertions on the part of my progressive readers. In imitation of those *Dutch Made Easy* or *Mathematics Is Fun* books, one could collect a few of the easier examples to make up a handbook that might be called *Gaullism Without Tears*. One of the characteristics of French cultured circles is to oversimplify complex questions and wrap simple ones in Byzantine subtleties. This way they avoid saying anything—even when engaged in the simple matter of conveying information—and yet give the impression of great cleverness. They bring vast resources to bear and employ logical and rhetorical tricks of staggering ingenuity to put across a couple of banal and erroneous ideas. They talk much about "economy of means," but under the circumstances they ought rather to boast of their economy of ends. The above description holds for the area of psychology as well as for that of criticism and politics. The refusal to face problems squarely is compounded by an ability to find elaborate solutions to nonexistent ones.

And so we get the simple formula for conversion to the Fifth Republic: whatever the Chief of State does right could have been wrought by no other political regime; whatever he botches would have been botched by any other political regime or, better, is the fault of the previous administration. To give an example, I recall being present in July, 1964, when

Valerie Giscard d'Estaing, the Minister of Finance and Economic Affairs, took the floor at the National Assembly during one of those rare sessions—distressing caricatures of parliamentary debates—whose only purpose is to permit the government to squelch a mythical opposition. The minister was discussing the question of meat, the price of which, despite a "stabilization program" that its promoters had praised to the skies, kept rising every day. A couple of timorous, stuttering "members of the opposition," probably chosen by straws for the dirty work, ventured to point this out. Then the minister drew himself up angrily, declaring that he would not "tolerate sarcastic animadversions" just because the price of beef had gone up "a couple of centimes" when the full responsibility for the increase lay with the Fourth Republic, which had given meat "bad structures" (for like everybody else the ministers of the Fifth Republic are "structuralists"). I admit that I raised my hat to this man. For here was the Fifth Republic, which by then had held absolute power for seven consecutive years, still crying, "Don't blame me, sir; it was the Fourth Republic's fault." The miracle is that the whole nation didn't burst out laughing (especially since the minister's speech was televised).

The nation just wasn't up to form that day; but from that moment on any dilations upon France's celebrated intelligence and critical spirit would, like its "Cartesian spirit" and "love of liberty," have to be reserved for textbooks dealing with our prehistory. Those "couple of centimes" were all the fault of the Fourth Republic! Why not of Louis the Sixteenth? Our authoritarian minister, like all authoritarian ministers, considers the past as the big villian, but what he didn't seem to realize was that *the past he was talking about also included himself*. Why should he have, when the Left itself was encouraging everyone to forget it? All dictatorships thrive on the "before us/after us" antithesis, for they are

36

founded on the mirage of a resurrection. The new Left's revolutionary contribution to this mania for renovation consists in creating a state of mind which holds that *it is rude to oppose the regime with valid, well-founded criticisms.* The Leftist editorial writer's heart hammers guiltily at the thought that he might be accused of "obsessional anti-Gaullism" and of love for the Fourth Republic whenever he happens to be struck by some governmental failure. He will call attention to the failure only if he can cloak his reference in a profusion of embarrassed circumlocutions designed to clear him of the suspicion of "partisanship." "I bow to my adversary," he always seems to say between the lines, "and do him homage. I deplore our differences of opinion, especially since no one is more qualified than he to put my program into effect. I will refrain from attacking him and criticizing him, for everyone knows that I disagree with him and hence might suspect me of axe grinding. Though I will avoid anything that might be construed as ill-temper, I must insist on expressing my disappointment at seeing once again, etc., etc., but I deliberately avoid arguments that might seem petty and which some people might seize on to exploit negatively."

Today in French Leftist circles "intellectual honesty" no longer means an impartial examination of the government's arguments, but rather the magnanimous suppression of the opposition's arguments by the self-same opposition. The methods whereby this very simple result was achieved are varied; they would baffle description if it were not for a certain underlying sameness in their banality.

Let us take the Algerian War as an example, for without the war the Fourth Republic might have finally developed into something truly republican and the Fifth would never have come into being. The war went on for something less than four years under the Fourth Republic and about the same amount of time under the Fifth. But each single one of these almost eight years was about twice as intense as its predecessor in terms of the exacerbation of the two sides, the increased intractability of the Army and of the Pieds Noirs, the lies fed to the public, the degeneration of our political customs, the growth of illegality, war crimes, the deterioration of our position in world affairs, financial waste, etc. When General de Gaulle took power, he promised a quick Algerian miracle; but the war was in fact to continue, and become very long and very dirty, and end not with a solution but with a convulsive, bloody collapse. This was undoubtedly due to the fact that the General had been carried to power by the extremists, who demanded a "French solution"; as a consequence, he was neither willing nor able to start negotiations during the first part of his administration, and had to wait until he was approached —no matter how long and costly the delay—once he had learned to his cost that negotiation was inevitable.

The informed opposition will object that de Gaulle was prepared to negotiate from the start (which is to give him the benefit of a doubt for which we have no grounds either in his past actions or in his speeches at the time) and that French public opinion was not ready to accept Algerian independence —which excuse was periodically offered under both the Fourth Republic and the Fifth by those who were unable to make the Army and the Pieds Noirs accept Paris policy. In fact, Guy Mollet and Mendès-France won the parliamentary elections of January, 1956, primarily on a platform of peace in Algeria, which came to nothing when Mollet capitulated after the Algerian riot; moreover, the polls show that de Gaulle's popularity reached its highest points in France after his speech of September, 1959 (in which he proposed self-determination for Algeria), and at the time of the putsch of April, 1961, when the army in Algeria defied the government and metropolitan France's desire for peace. Therefore, the country was not against negotiation; indeed, in January, 1961, it had given de Gaulle full authority to go ahead. If he did not do so, it was because he was opposed by the same enemies of the popular will who first forced the Fourth Republic to pursue policies contrary to those for which it had been elected and then destroyed it.

The reason de Gaulle was not also destroyed was that his enemies could put up no champion of their own to match him. But although he did not fall, neither could he solve the Algerian question as the nation wanted it solved; he had to wait until events spoke for themselves and the army's collapse into bloody anarchy drove the French in Algeria back to metropolitan France. And here the informed opposition will tell you that the Fourth Republic had failed to settle the Algerian question. If you protest that you're perfectly well aware of that fact because you too were a bitter opponent of the Fourth Republic's colonial policy, if you add that all the colonial wars—Indochina, Tunisia, Morocco—ended in hellish chaos because of pigheadedness and vacillating and contradictory policies and that the Algerian War was no exception, and finally that the settlement, fine as it was, was not worth the sacrifice of what was left of our democratic institutions, you will be told that in any case peace was concluded under de Gaulle, not under the Fourth Republic. Absolutely right—and it wasn't concluded under Pepin the Short, either. Time is of the essence in politics, particularly during those regimes in which you do not have to achieve anything in order to remain in power. And, by the same token, shouldn't the Fourth Republic receive credit for the treaties signed during its regime in just as bad and sometimes much better conditions? And shouldn't we give bad marks to de Gaulle for having in 1945 oriented the Indochinese War toward total reconquest? No, for he was only continuing the colonialist tradition of the Third Republic, and in 1945 "no one" (*sic*) could have foreseen that the Empire would have to be sacrificed.

The interesting thing is not that the above exchange took

place but that it took place (as I have often noticed) between two people who both claim to be anti-Gaullist. What is astonishing is that one of the speakers, under the pretext of impartiality and extremely subtle political analysis, is far craftier in camouflaging the contradictions, incoherence and ineffectiveness of Gaullist policies than are the party propagandists. The really honest thing for him to do would be to join the official party; but one senses that in many cases like his only fear of what people would say, a desire to continue to be considered "men of the Left" (who today would dare proclaim himself to be "of the right"?), the pull of a Leftist mystique that goes back to the Popular Front and the Resistance, an unwillingness to break with the "Marxist" lives that they had led with such blind faith, prevent these sheepish crypto-Gaullists from moving bag and baggage into the stronger party.

When you do not share the Gaullist's views, he tricks you into becoming an "unconditional" supporter of the Fourth Republic—even though you may have been in almost complete disagreement with its policies—which lumps you together with the "obsessional" anti-Gaullists (these two adjectives play a large role in a political vocabulary that is growing more impoverished every day). It is useless to tell him that as far as you are concerned the Fifth Republic is only the Fourth pursued with different means and with the suppression of those legal safeguards which one could in other periods insist be honored. Nothing will get through to him: whatever goes badly under de Gaulle would have gone just as badly if the Fourth Republic had continued; whatever succeeds under him would have failed under another man or not even been attempted. That is the argument you've got to be prepared for. At any rate, de Gaulle has held absolute power for so long that it is impossible either to prove or even come close to disproving these arguments by reasonable evidence. The reasoning of love—which transforms even the faults of a mistress into virtues in her lover's eyes—is the reasoning of the sheepish Gaullists, and it is especially effective on their lips because the harem of the Fifth Republic contains but one nautch girl, and she personally chooses the eunuchs who will watch over her. It is the same kind of reasoning we saw at work when we were dealing with Algerian policy, and we could give other examples of its wondrous results in foreign policy, in educational and cultural policy or in economic and financial policy.

Before I take up these various areas, so rich in lessons, where shines the spirit of opposition—and spiritual opposition —I feel that I must answer an objection which has undoubtedly occurred to many readers. Haven't the intellectuals, you object, and professors in particular, been almost by definition constantly anti-Gaullist? Indeed, could we not even reproach them, on the contrary, for having accepted a sketchy definition of the Right and a no less sketchy one of the Left and of what divides them? And of not having been willing to acknowledge the objectively progressive role the Fifth Republic played in its fight against the Right-wing colonialists and militarists, in its diplomatic recognition of Communist China and in certain aspects of its economic and cultural planning? Isn't it absurd to portray the French intelligentsia as prey to conservatism and conformity when it seems on the contrary to have often lacked impartiality because of its traditional attachment to an emotional Leftism not unlike "Rightist anarchism?" Aren't the Gaullists right to throw it into the teeth of progressives that de Gaulle "kept other people's promises," to revive Pétain's slogan?

All this is true. Or, rather, it is true that most intellectuals are "potentially" or in principle anti-Gaullist through emotional commitment, and that under certain circumstances they will proclaim it with loud huzzas. But it is also true that they believe they are in the wrong, that they violently reproach one another for their sterile partisanship in fighting the regime, that they say one thing when they talk and another when they write for publication and that they are adapting themselves happily to the regime and to the society that created it. The verbal objections that they raise are both feeble and vaguely Leftist, while the way in which they adapt to reality is energetic, fruitful and discreet. They labor under a feeling that "the Left has failed," which stems from the fact that most of them are former Marxists who decided that Marxism can no longer be applied to prosperous industrial societies. Precisely because of their naïve Marxist indoctrination, they are loath to defend the "purely juridical and formal liberties" of "bourgeois liberalism" and so fall into the most obvious pitfalls of a liberal empire. What pride they have left keeps them from openly supporting it (God knows what they do when they vote); they become either caricatures of an antiquated Left whom the Minister of the Interior ought to subsidize (which he does indirectly in some cases) or sages whose tortuous analyses start with mental confusion and end with moral and political passivity. In fact, the common denominator of their analytical essays is that the conclusions contradict the evidence adduced to support them. The latter is essentially conservative and coincides with the aspirations of the Fifth Republic; but the conclusions show a writer who reasserts his Leftist origins. The Fifth Republic aspires to a lower-middle-class ideal which has been cleverly made to serve the upper-middle class: prosperity through inequality, but controlled and disguised so that it is never so great as to cause any serious discontent; mediocrity and security within an absurd economy; nationalistic exaltation under so xenophobic a foreign policy that it verges on megalomania, whose ridiculous failures are carefully hidden from the public, which, in any case, is so ill-informed that it does not notice—let alone judge—what goes on. Basically in agreement with this policy, our men of the Left wake from their dazzling daydreams only long enough to utter casually and unconvincingly the periodic, revolutionary cry that their faithful clientele expects.

What has happened? France has always had a powerful reactionary current that never acknowledged democracy—to say nothing of the equality of all citizens before the law—and that for over a hundred and fifty years has stubbornly challenged the political principles of the First French Revolution. Opposed to it, France has the intellectuals of the Left—their sights fixed on the second revolution, the economic and social one—who have learned mostly to criticize the hypocrisy of bourgeois parliamentary institutions and, like Marx, to insist that purely political democracy is not enough—with the pretty result that they have not only failed to bring about the Second Revolution, but have also destroyed a good part of the First. Strangely insensitive to violations of civil liberties and abuses of power, they do not seem to understand that the establishment of arbitrary power, and the resulting incapacity of the Frenchman today to invoke effectively any article of the law if the government has decided otherwise, constitute a much more serious historical regression than would an electoral victory of the Conservatives in England or of the Republicans in the United States.

They are extremely susceptible to the economic aspects of the state of affairs today, but they forget that no modern state in an industrialized country would be willing or able to do away with social security, retirement, planning, the organization of credit and the regulation of economic growth. To oh and ah over Planning as a sign of progressiveness is as naïve as it would be to credit the Gaullist renovation of our institutions with the railroads and electricity. No regime now has a monopoly on technocracy. If we mistake the gains attributable to our epoch for those of the state under which we happen to live, are we not swallowing one of the most common lies of Rightist demagogy? Hitler's Germany did not permit corporal punishment in its schools as did free England in the nineteenth century. We must revive the old idea that there exists a general state of customs, with advances and retreats, that is in the short run independent of political tendencies. The lot of the working classes has improved in the whole of Western Europe during the last hundred years under all kinds of regimes, but this does not mean that it was just as good to live under one regime as under another, or that they all honored human dignity to the same extent. The workingman was better treated in Fascist Italy than in Victorian England, but the credit goes to the twentieth century, not to Fascism. All the industrial peoples of our time are likely to be well nourished, educated, motorized, socially insured, pensioned, cultured and asphyxiated; the only difference between them will consist in the fact that some will be intelligent and others idiots, some politically free and others treated like children, and that some will regulate their own conduct while others will have it regulated for them by the wife of the Chief of State.

Moreover, it is interesting to note that progressives and Marxists have succumbed more readily to Gaullist propaganda than the traditionally republican Center-Left. This is because the progressives and Marxists have yielded to the charms of neo-capitalistic economic planning, which oddly enough they refuse to realize tends to aggravate economic injustice; they have also been seduced by several *coups d'éclat* in foreign policy, which gratified an anti-Americanism that dates back to the Marshall Plan and the Korean War. The traditionally republican Center-Left, on the other hand, is the spiritual heir of political principles more than two centuries old, principles to which it is genuinely attached, and not because it is eager to jump on some bandwagon. It must be emphasized that both of these are bourgeois currents. The working masses—whether

44

Socialist, Communist or Christian-Democrat—have long since abandoned any attempts at political thinking, and have taken refuge in a timorous conformism that doesn't even amount to reformism, because the workers are content to be tossed the bone of occasional pay raises and do not link their demands to a reform of institutions or of the economic system. Never have the French working classes and the "economically under-privileged" been so far from understanding their true political situation as they are today. The sixty-five-year-old maid who is reduced to sleeping with the Sisters of Charity for one franc a night campaigns militantly for her local Communist cell and then votes in favor of personal power at the referendum. The members of the opposition, like the men in power, offer their followers cover-ups, not explanations: when they want them to do a certain thing, they put forward irrelevant reasons.

Early in 1960, pretending that they did not want to be thought of as "doctrinaire," they suddenly discovered that the Fifth Republic had certain virtues; but what they were really doing was getting the masses psychologically prepared for Khrushchev's official visit to France. Not for a second did they think of giving an honest explanation for the visit, which they could easily have justified without trying to justify Gaullism too. For them the realistic thing to do is to brainwash the electorate and deprive it of its political bearings—and then they're surprised when even cleverer propagandists profit by the electorate's lack of bearings. They have forgotten the great call of the nineteenth century: to educate the masses. In those days, bourgeois intellectuals devoted to the cause of justice bypassed the official organs of information and addressed the people directly, providing those elements of education and philosophy that the official school system and news media would not supply. Apparently the glamour of the Nazi, Fascist and Stalinist regimes has definitively caused propaganda to be accepted as the only means of political expression. Propaganda being the art of making people go in a certain direction without telling them where they're going, and of finding words and images instead of sound reasons to make them go that way without giving them a general picture of your aims and how you propose to accomplish them, the trick quickly becomes one of trying to start political ground swells by inventing aims that have nothing to do with what you are really after. Even when it might be advantageous for them to play a winning card by simply and clearly speaking their minds, modern politicians prefer to go down in defeat under some clever propaganda slogan, like those shifty businessmen who through inclination and habit prefer to lose money in an underhanded deal rather than make it honestly. It may be that, no matter what their political coloring, politicians are motivated primarily by the need to distinguish themselves as a class from the rest of humanity, to perpetuate the myth that *political* intelligence differs from ordinary intelligence, not only by virtue of its specialized knowledge, but also in certain eternal, internal qualities.

All of which is not straying from my subject, for what best explains de Gaulle's seduction of the Left is his consummate acting of the role of "political thinker": empty-headed, contradictory, demagogic, authoritarian and mysterious. The Communists saw themselves beaten by a propaganda that was even more effective than theirs; but they were forced to grudging admiration because "mounting propaganda campaigns" had been their own principal stock in trade ever since the war. The progressives—that is, the bourgeois intellectuals of the Left—having no faithful to lead or doctrines to follow, went their own way.

Not for them the orgies of propaganda but the solitary joys of analysis. Unfortunately, whenever the Fifth Republic did something that any democrat could approve of (like the belated treaty in Algeria), they "analyzed" favorably; but when it came to criticizing the regime, they clammed up and grew glum. For instance, in July, 1961, Bourguiba reminded the French that they still had not evacuated Bizerte as they were committed to by treaty. To this insult the French replied with a merciless attack on the defenseless Tunisians. Several hundred dead and atrocities which journalists from all over the world witnessed. All this occurred in peacetime, and it is typical of the murderous and barbaric way in which the French assert their virile vocation, which is to wage war—but never, if possible, against an army. And what did de Gaulle do? There is no doubt that the order to be "firm" came from him. At any rate, he did nothing either to stop the massacre or to deny it. And what did the opposition do? Nothing. A slaughter which under the Third Republic (but not under the Fourth, because everybody was already afraid of the Gaullists) would have shamefully brought down the government went almost unnoticed by the opposition. True, at that time of year, the flower of our proletarian youth, the Leftist intelligentsia, was laboring selflessly in Saint-Tropez, Ramatuelle, Gassin (or in Yugoslavia, or in some "little trattoria in Trastevere" . . .).

Let the reader who has had the patience to read this far, or the good luck to open the book at this point, take heart: I am not going to cram him with the dull stuff of French history, for France is utterly without interest. In the modern world, it is the also-ran among nations. Considered as an example of a pre-industrial civilization, it is without any real touristic or ethnographic appeal. It cannot qualify in terms of modernity, and such antiquities as it possesses are comparatively modern. As it is neither the United States nor Sicily, it offers only a flavorless cosmopolitanism, in which laundromats exist side by side with dirty wash, and the main problem is the extension and proliferation of telephone wires—which will enable many more conversations to take place but won't raise their level. An egoistic people, tight-fisted, eternally ill-tempered, hashing over its gory war exploits, that are as dull as the murders of unimportant kinglets in Shakespeare; a mere province with delusions of grandeur topped off with sham politics, where the latest trick is to vote first, in order to have the right later to read the papers and learn what the government's program is; a country which does not even have the fancy of madness or the wisdom of mediocrity, but which at least once had a few standards and moral codes, one of which under various forms never included resignation and coward-liness—the French people have lost their characteristic vigi-lance and have become once again bumpkins of immeasurable credulity.

And the intellectuals, who never up to now sided with the sources of power except by accident (or, rather, only when the sources of power came round to their point of view), have now been replaced by a new breed that makes a *real vocation* out of agreeing with the established civil, military, university and religious authorities, regardless of who they are or what their program. My point is not to praise one attitude or the other: I am only saying that the old-line French intellectual (let's say until 1940) generally mistrusted both the powers that be and the society around him, and felt somewhat uneasy if by chance he found himself in agreement with the judgments, tastes, prejudices or way of life of the middle and upper classes, and that today the opposite is true: whenever he finds himself in disagreement or approaching things "nega-tively," he gets worried and is assailed by self-doubt; he feels ill at ease and aspires with the whole of his being to be at one with those in power, to merge with the majority. In order to illustrate this point, I shall adduce a number of examples, which will inevitably prove very boring; for France and its politics are boring; French intellectuals, whose reasoning is both very dense and at the same time very lightweight, are boring; the keepers of the State are boring, as are their speeches, acts and ceremonies, not to mention the people which constitute their public, including this people's way of life, its problems and the way it resolves them, together with its work, leisure and culture. So please you, concede therefore that it would be impossible for me to write a *Marriage of Figaro* for you when the libretto was written jointly by Paul Claudel and Marshal Foch. Oh, I know, France is a country that takes getting used to. And if I had to, I could get everything I think about France into three pages (see Summary at the end of this volume), but, not unnaturally, people demand proof, even if it seems pointless to give it to them, since proof has absolutely no effect on the French. Nevertheless, one has to go into all the dull details of our national life, the way in which our minds work, our pride, our laziness, our dreary society without generosity or surprises, our calculated emotions and our thinking that is determined solely by the interests of the tribe and of getting ahead. Oh well, narcissism saves bores from their own boredom. And it is narcissism, too, that transfigures the tenuous thread of local legends into the inexhaustible flood of the epic.

Since the Frenchman is my subject and the source of my inspiration for these divagations, I shall exercise my right as a French citizen to belabor him with a few more examples, which I shall develop at some length and treat from every conceivable angle. Each will throw light upon the spontaneous degeneration of our people and its thinkers. Here is the list of examples—you can skip the ones that don't interest you, though I warn you that I am not going to take them up in the order here given: (1) the economic policy of France since 1958; (2) student demonstrations and the repression thereof; (3) the Manifesto of the 121; (4) the timorous, admiring and jealous rapture of the modern French intellectual before the so-called "man of action"—any kind: bankers, oil field roustabouts, pipe fitters, chauffeurs, airport control tower operators, flagpole sitters, boatmen; it doesn't matter what kind. True, each occupation may individually be very educational and perhaps even lucrative, but according to what I've been hearing lately such activities are somehow indispensable to abstract thought, poetry and morality. This is a new attitude, and it dates, to be precise, from Malraux and Saint-Exupéry (forgive me for using names that will be meaningless in fifty years; the reader in the year 2020 will have to understand that I was writing in an age when France was not burgeoning with geniuses of world renown). Now, let's say you play tennis; it does your general health a world of good and tones up your muscles; besides you like it. But that's not enough: you think better and more incisively for playing it. Indeed, you render yourself more *worthy* of thinking. Why? Because the exercise eliminated the toxins from your body? Of course not! What a pedestrian and scientific explanation! The reason is that Action in and of itself is midwife to Thought. You *prove to yourself* that you can play tennis (no point in proving it to anyone else) and that makes you a man of action; ergo, you think. Or take a machine gun. Someone attacks you; you defend yourself. Is that all that happens? Of course not! The minute you go "bang-bang," you reach a level of being which embraces both the active and the contemplative life. If you don't go "bang-bang" fast enough and the other chap goes "bang-bang" first, you have just had the boon of "sacrifice" bestowed upon you (the concept of sacrifice is at once military, religious and personal-literary); and this boon permits you to "realize yourself fully" (for a brief moment, of course, but well worth the bother), provided you "assume it lucidly" and so "seize your own destiny."

The only reason that those who preach such shocking drivel are not immediately invited to practice what they preach is that by tradition we have a high regard for "divine war." Take Bigeard,[9] for example. Like all paratroopers, Bigeard was a great hiker; his name means nothing today, but just be patient. Not only did he invent a particular type of helmet, which has earned him the undying devotion of part of our youth, he also "invented a specialty" (I use the words of the legend) that was all his own: that of killing his adversaries *respectfully*. He acquired a modicum of fame by "paying his compliments" to various corpses. Then the inevitable happened: he wrote a book. Its very title, *No Beast in the World*, intimated that it was a plea for human spirituality, quasi-divine and Teilhardized (this adjective will be unintelligible in 2020; but what the devil, the people who write theses and introductions have to have something to annotate), which all but advocated self-transcendence by means of murder and photography and thrilled our adventure writers to their very marrow. The disciples of Malraux, like devotees at avant-garde concerts, applauded noisily and cast a challenging eye about them, but disappointingly enough everyone was irreproachably docile. Needless to say, it is these sons of Malraux and Lawrence (the active, or French, Lawrence—T.E., not D.H.) who make up the Leftist intelligentsia.

From 1955 to 1962, while countries lacking our grandeur were childishly announcing biological discoveries and the launching of rockets and satellites, France was in the position of announcing daily that a certain number of rebels had been "slaughtered." This expression, incidentally, was hastily emended in the daily news bulletins of the French radio and television network. It must have grated on the delicate ears of certain persons to whom the word "slaughter" seemed too

[9] Colonel Marcel Bigeard was born in 1916. Taken prisoner during World War II, he escaped and fought in the Resistance. After the war, Colonel Bigeard served in Indochina (where he was again taken prisoner) and Algeria. Since 1956 he has been in command of several paratroop formations.—*Translator's note.*

harsh and brutish for France, especially when what you ought to do is to emphasize that your adversaries are not insignificant. Accordingly, subsequent newscasts were adorned with such expressions as "from the operational point of view" and "operational balance sheet." "From the operational point of view" meant "How many did we kill?" and "operational balance sheet" was "the number of corpses." After 1962, having no one left to slaughter, France concentrated on its nuclear deterrent, which soon came to absorb an enormous part of the budget (presented so misleadingly that it was difficult to figure out how disproportionate was the amount set aside for the development of a French bomb—still another example of how our democracy is founded on respect for an enlightened citizenry).

Note that out of all the vast areas available for unproductive investment France inevitably chose the military. Or, rather, it chose the only area that is completely and eternally unproductive, not just unproductive in the short run. Neither scientific research nor the proposed educational reform that the last ministers of education of the Fourth Republic drew up in 1956 and 1957—a reform which would have been the first experiment of its kind in history and which the whole world would have considered truly original—got any of the big money, which started to jingle with joy at the mere prospect of exploding our dirty bomb. Another point, and very typical: when the 1965 budget was debated, the French Left did not say that it would renounce the nuclear deterrent if it came to power—which proves once again that all Frenchmen have become alike.

You could see it coming some years back, when the Left scarcely bothered to disguise its admiration for action and the army, just before the successful putsch of 1958. The palpitations that Bigeard's book aroused were but one example of this admiration. During the same years the newspapers of the Left and Center were crammed with articles entitled "On the Military Mind" or "Intellectuals and the Military." The point of all these articles, not to mention books, was to prove that the Leftist intellectuals' hostility to the tortures in Algeria, for instance, was not to be taken as hostility to everything military. Starting from the premise that there is a military reality, which is no less a part of the human condition than the agricultural, artistic and scientific realities, or than maternity and sexuality, and accepting the idea that there is a distinction between the "military" and the "intellectual"—as one makes a distinction between manual labor and office work when one wishes to demonstrate that neither is inferior to the other—the Left merely surrendered to its secret admiration for the most reactionary values of military supremacy, which constitute the great failing of the French. Among the numerous articles that I have clipped from the newspapers of the period, I cite one at random.

It is a short letter that appeared in *Le Monde* of April 4, 1958, and was written by a man who did a very great deal to expose the use of torture in Algeria without being able to do anything to stop it, because, like so many other well-meaning souls, he wanted to expose torture without rejecting the army, without proclaiming that the institution itself is fundamentally evil and that humanity will not be human until the day that the memory of what an army is has faded from the face of the earth. In his letter Pierre-Henri Simon wrote, with reference to the term "slaughtered rebels": "I wish that I had read at least one protest against an expression that frequently occurs in the press and sometimes also in military communiqués: 'So-and-so-many rebels were *slaughtered.*' One slaughters an animal, but one kills a man. True, the police 'slaughter' a criminal, which means that his crime has separated him from humanity; but this is strictly a word that policemen use, not soldiers. . . . The Algerian lad, however, who hides in the *djebel* because of his ideals and who, trapped by an enemy superior both in numbers and arms, has little chance of escaping . . . this boy, who is seldom more than sixteen or seventeen years old, is a rebel, yes; but he is also a soldier." What all this means is that the Algerian revolutionary is worthy of being "killed" and not "slaughtered" *because he is a soldier.* Mr. Simon is seeking not to convince the French army that its "cause" amounts to no more than murder in the name of grocers, cops and putschists, but to demand that the Arab be treated in accordance with military statutes, to sprinkle a little chivalric perfume (imported from France) on the sun-blackened body of the ex-farmhand. Following M. Simon, Jean Planchais, in *Le Monde* of March 18, 1959, describes —with reference to Bigeard—"the immense sadness on the evening after victory, that deep sense of solidarity which goes out and embraces even the enemy." He adds: "Death is the only conclusion; the hero has no other future." This is all very well, but at present Bigeard is in good health and, as far as his future is concerned, I read somewhere the other day that he was up for promotion to the rank of general.

In the same article, M. Planchais wrote that "this primitive ideal is . . . the very antithesis of literature," while in fact it is nothing but literature. And even theology, for Bigeard says of his hero: "It was his way of envisioning God." And there you have the intellectual and moral heritage of France, A.D. 1965: Saint-Exupéry, Malraux, Teilhard de Chardin, Bigeard.

One can understand the political destiny and the psychological climate of present-day France only if one realizes that in the last few years and for the first time in their history the French—all the French—believe in the same things, love the same things, respect and admire the same things and aspire to be the same thing. In brief, what makes the present period so exciting for those who love this sort of thing, is that France is a changing country; in fact, it has already become *another country.* I am speaking in a moral sense, which is all that interests me; as I see it, all countries are more or less the same as far as steam irons and air conditioners are concerned. The only French peculiarity worth noting in this respect is that France has all the psychological ills of the so-called gadget civilization—without having this civilization itself. Everything breaks down in France, where more than anywhere else you get technical progress rammed down your throat at every opportunity. True, for an appliance to break down, it must first have been constructed and installed; in this sense, then, breakdowns can be considered a sign of modernization. But that is not the point, for sooner or later even we Frenchmen will manage to make our appliances work. No, the real point is that modernization is the same everywhere, but men and nations are not. They were not the same when they lived in squalor; they are not the same when they live in luxury.

It is striking that most of the Leftist protests against torture were based on a conservative view of things, that is, they took alleged military ideals literally and thought that urging professional soldiers to respect a code of martial purity, supposedly ingrained in the military mind, but which has never existed in any army in the world, would be a crafty maneuver. "War is a tough, cruel game," wrote Pierre-Henri Simon in *Le Monde* on May 30, 1957, "but it is possible to play it like a man." An entire civilization hangs by this sentence. The moment one subscribes to this idea, it is futile to argue about how far you can go. For extremists will always go further than moderates, even though they have the same principles. Simon continues, "By nature, the soldier is closer to the knight than to the policeman, but even the latter is by no means necessarily inhuman." After making such statements, how could one hope to prevent or curb atrocities that were committed and excused in the name of a moral system that one basically adhered to oneself? It is hardly astonishing that, two years later, the same writer (*Le Monde*, January 30, 1959) was still asking for a dialogue between the military and the intellectuals: "If we wish to avoid the difficulties, refine the motives and overcome the contradictions inherent in an ideological war, a dialogue between our military men and intellectuals is in order." To label the Algerian War "ideological" proves that the idealization of the real is going great guns in twentieth-century France.

First of all, there is not—nor has been nor will nor can be—such a thing as an ideological war, unless you consider that crematory ovens are an ideological operation on the grounds that they are based on the *idea* of racism. So then what point is there in asking the directors of Auschwitz if it wouldn't perhaps be possible—without, of course, ceasing their activity—to avoid its difficulties or at least to "refine the motives" and "overcome the inherent contradictions"? To admit that these gentlemen are the victims of contradictions is to admit that their activity, legitimate in theory, merely has flaws in its application. And, if you admit this, you basically agree with them, however honest your intentions may be. This was the case of the Left generally—and of a Left by courtesy that was often much more extremist than *Le Monde*. In short, although some were motivated by their devotion to the traditional values of military patriotism and to the memory of our great writers who fell on the field of battle—Péguy, Psichari, Alain Fournier, Saint-Exupéry and others—by an aesthetic of action and adventure that they took from Malraux, all showed that they could not escape the spell of the age-old rhetoric that tells us that it is noble to kill and to be killed. I have dwelt on now-forgotten events and controversies only in order to show how the French Left, even when it protested most bitterly, had at this early date secretly started to accept a Rightist view of the state—and this will clarify what is to follow.

If additional proof were required to show what side most of the Left took at that time—the worst moment in the aging crisis that was the Algerian War—one could find no finer example than the famous Manifesto of the 121. The reader will recall that in 1960 a number of writers and intellectuals—121 to begin with and 180 or 200 at the end—mailed a manifesto in sealed envelopes to various government officials, particularly judges, calling their kind attention to the war crimes being committed in Algeria (which were so well known to the recipients that there was no need to enumerate them) and postulating the French soldier's "right to disobey in the Algerian War." I will not go through the whole story (such narratives are inevitably tedious) but will content myself with extracting the lessons that are pertinent to my argument. While the government did do its duty and gave the affair maximum publicity with its clumsy accusations—even though no trial could have been staged without blowing up in the prosecution's face and furnishing the accused with a providential tribune—official anger was nevertheless truly moderate compared to that of the Leftist circles politically close to the signers. We will omit the Communists, who, as I mentioned earlier, could always dig up some text from Lenin stating that the revolutionary soldier's first duty is to infiltrate the torturers' camp and work doubly hard to help them. Let us focus, instead, on the furious reaction of the non-Communist Left and its organs. Not only did they denounce the Manifesto as unrealistic and politically immature, but they even went so far as to play it up in their papers as an overt attempt to incite the soldiers to mutiny, and on those grounds they condemned it. Now, this Manifesto was not addressed to soldiers; it was not pasted on barrack-room walls; it was addressed to individuals in the form of personal letters. I grant that this offered a legal loophole—although the signers probably didn't realize it at the time; in any case, it gave them the excuse that they had not, strictly speaking, intended to incite soldiers to mutiny but to encourage badly informed authorities to be favorably disposed toward soldiers who were disobeying of their own free will because the Algerian War was what it was. The Rightist press did its bit to insure that the text was interpreted as a genuine incitement to mutiny, and not as a general postulate of a right to disobey. But did the Leftist press have to take the same position? Did it have to commend some of its own colleagues (for most of the signers of the Manifesto were journalists) to the zealous hands of the examining magistrates? Did it have to be in such an indecent hurry to put the noose about their necks? Why did journalists and politicians of the Left suddenly subject their friends to an implacable hatred and harshness of tone, only a fraction of which would have been very useful had it been directed against the powers that be?

Simply because the Manifesto had hit home and was a most humiliating bill of indictment against the French Left rather than a cause of preoccupation to the government, for our leaders knew that the 1960-style French private, a tiny mustached racist addicted to comic books and pin-ups, was not exactly cut out for disobedience.

It is easy to understand how it came about that this sharp criticism of governmental policy turned the Left's stomach instead of arousing its appetite. After all, for some years the Left had been proclaiming that its mistake had been to nourish itself on memories of the movement during the nineteenth century and the Popular Front of 1936 and on the illusion that another "Great Dawn" would come and bring them victory. First, they argued, they should admit that there were positive sides to the government's policies and that they should openly acknowledge them as such and stop making an obsession of their ridiculous extremism. And it must be said that the Left demonstrated an unusual verve in pursuing this part of its new course—that is, in doing justice to what it thought were the positive aspects of the governmental policy. It was imperative, they continued, to penetrate the complex structures of the present-day world, to avoid falling into disrepute through a generally negative attitude, and to comprehend through reason and dissect through analysis what the state, the economy, religion, the functions of force and of the police really are, so as to win the adversary's respect rather than bring about his overthrow, and also to enlighten rather than arm the militant revolutionary. Hadn't intransigence got them nowhere? Enough of these theoretical scruples, wafty plans and fruitless revolts. Like Gaullist France, the Left had to "wed its epoch," that is, wed the Right, since its epoch was France and France was the Right.

Unfortunately, thousands of pages of analysis—of which the least that can be said is that they hardly prompted the reader to hasty conclusions or rash decisions—failed either to influence the government or to attract readers and militant Leftists. And now, lo and behold, there appears on the scene the most "romantic" and spontaneous of manifestoes, completely free from any considerations of short-term effectiveness and absolutely foreign to the supposed aspirations of the "affluent society." It simply expressed an emotional reaction to, a moral demand on and a physical revulsion for the leaders and their creatures; and it stirred up a national storm, forced the government to take measures that it had to drop (it hardly cared to haul André Breton or Jean-Paul Sartre into court to state their views on the Algerian War in front of journalists of all nationalities), attracted the attention of the world to France and made the front pages from England and Mexico to Switzerland and India. What the most diligent editorialists of the Left had vainly tried to accomplish week after week—to bring the pressure of world opinion to bear on the French government—had been accomplished by a bunch of hysterical whippersnappers in a tirade that contained not a jot of serious analysis of the objective situation! A threefold humiliation: the amateurs had beaten the pros; the scholarly Left had had it proved to them that its timorous approach was not paying off and that its calculations were erroneous; and, finally, the repercussions of the Manifesto of the 121, a slap in the face to this ineffectual Left that never once aroused public opinion under the Fifth Republic, had unmasked our Leftists for the sheepish Gaullists they had become. The event showed that their lack of aggressiveness was a mistake, and that their policy of moderation had been motivated not by hope of gain—which, in any case, had failed to materialize—but by a deeply rooted sympathy for the Gaullist regime.

The first job of an opposition is not to analyze but to react, for there comes a point when one just can't stand certain things and faces any longer. This may not be all there is to opposition, but it is the *sine qua non* for any effective action under a dictatorial regime. The very impotence of those who are right proves that the rulers are wrong. The reaction of the Left as a whole to the Manifesto of the 121 showed how ignorant it was of the existence of whole areas of indignation, which it imagined had disappeared merely because it could not manage to rouse them with its sorry arguments. And it demonstrated, moreover, how much the Left had absorbed of the old-fogy attitude, which holds that the revolution should find its niche within the given situation and its internal structures, instead of attacking from without.

The French ex-Left has rejected active opposition for the sake of what it believes is a modern realism. In its view, an act like that of the 121, however effective it may be in stirring up sluggish public opinion and indifferent government officials, would keep France "perpetually in the nineteenth century." Let us see, then, how the Left today acts when it has to deal with the twentieth century and those areas that are of such vital importance to the future, such as education and economic planning. But first, two remarks. To these progressive thinkers, our President's way of life—so like that of a German princeling, what with its official receptions (mistaken for "politics in the grand manner")—doesn't in the least keep France "perpetually in the nineteenth century." On the other hand, they think that a street demonstration for peace in Algeria or a strike to force reforms in education does keep us there, as I myself have heard in the diminishing but diehard circles of the partisans of direct inaction. The spontaneous emotional choice implied by this distinction is very disturbing.[10] Second observation: alongside the flabby Left, which spends its time wondering how not to be unfair to technocracy and the holders of personal power, there was and still is a more active Left whose programs are so unrealizable that agitating for them in no way commits their authors. They dreamed of basing a social revolution in France on the Algerian underground, of putting Fidel Castro in charge of the French economy and, in the near future, of aiding the Vietcong, the natives of Angola and the blacks of South Africa through their words and writings (when words and writings are totally ineffective in France, especially against abuses of power and official propaganda).

These dreams are just an alibi, a conjurer's hocus-pocus to exorcise symbolically the guilt that they feel because they are enjoying all the good things of our affluent society. Besides, I have seen many well-meaning individuals change abruptly from frenzied revolutionaries into lethargic admirers of the President-General. And it is not in the least astonishing, for the two rival branches of the Left complement one another. Whenever the extremist minority does organize some sort of protest, the sheeplike majority invokes common sense

[10] No sooner does a strike promise to be successful than the Left starts worrying that it may be unpopular. No one bothers to ask if the government is "inconveniencing the public" when, with its characteristic contempt for the citizen, it orders the police to prevent cars from parking along main thoroughfares in Paris for two days, for the sole purpose of insuring that everyone will have a good view of an official parade—and stops traffic entirely during the rush hours when the parade is actually passing.

—pardon, an analysis of the structures of the modern world—in order to split any solidarity in the ranks of the opposition and, more important still, to dissociate itself from all antigovernmental actions the moment that they seem likely to prove successful. This is what happened in the case of the 121, for this Manifesto, which was unanimously condemned by the Leftist press, could hardly be termed unrealistic, unless it is unrealistic to point out that the best defense of those young Frenchmen sent out to serve a handful of colonials and colonels is, after all, disobedience. Indeed, it was so realistic and so simple that the government had a hard time convincing the Left that the French public, addicted to transistors and TV sets, was essentially stupid—as no one knew better than the government, for it was responsible for the condition. But ultimately the government was able to calm the Left, which had been panic-stricken at the thought that there might be a ruckus and that insurrections, trials, imprisonments, flights into exile—in short, "a perpetual nineteenth century"—might endanger the majestic course of its weekly editorials, which had grown increasingly long, increasingly obscure and less and less read outside the ministerial offices in which the material of their lucubrations originated.

The two French Lefts are, then, indispensable to one another. The extremist Left, by its very excesses in formulating political positions that are often worth attention in themselves but have no visible relation to the internal situation in France, gives the mild Leftists a pretext for condemning its stands on the nuclear deterrent, our economy, education and basic liberties as both utopian and old-fashioned, when they could not be more real and up-to-date. The extremist Left forgets that one cannot impose respect for human dignity on the world when one cannot obtain it at home. The mild Left uses this error as an excuse for not demanding it anywhere. You can make it swallow anything, since its basic principles are that parliamentarism is outdated—hence, the legislative branch can no longer exercise control over the executive one—that most strikes can be ascribed to "a perpetual nineteenth-century" mentality and that street demonstrations show a lack of political maturity. Moreover, the government laughs at press campaigns, which are transformed by self-censorship into lullabies when not into stirring "Marseillaises," neutralized by state television. The result is that there is no way in which to bring pressure to bear on the government. Also, the Left gets angry when someone has the courage to try something that may prove the contrary, and hastens to abandon him for fear that he might succeed.

Nothing is more striking than the way the Left turns tail, than its art of shutting its eyes, its frustrated anger not unlike that of the racetrack tout when a dark horse wins. And so the Left begins to sulk and look preoccupied when a specific battle looms in which the opposition holds all the trumps: defending a cause that is vital to the future, being ridiculed for trying to gain their point through negotiation, asking nothing impossible and deciding on strikes or demonstrations in order to obtain it. When the miners of Creusot go on strike, the Left is the first to proclaim that their demands are "old-fashioned" and serve to keep marginal enterprises alive artificially—as though the workers should transform themselves into economic planners and, in the light of the figures, decide to adjust their standard of living in accordance with the increase in national income. When it comes, however, to the students and the murderously inadequate budget for education, the Left can hardly claim that demanding buildings, laboratories, professors and libraries is a Malthusian error. And when these students demonstrate in the streets, no one says anything about it because it has been decreed that from now on there shall be no more street demonstrations. And when the government has the students clubbed, the Left gets mad . . . at the students, for it has been decreed that Gaullism is not Fascism, which is perfectly true until someone attacks it. In order to prove that it is not Fascism—and it has been so proven—one must therefore never attack it.

One day early in November, 1963, as I was passing through Saint-Germain-des-Prés, the Odéon intersection and the Latin Quarter, I was astonished to see what vast numbers of police and helmeted soldiers had massed there since morning. White ambulances with huge red crosses bore eloquent testimony to the Minister of the Interior's steadfastness of purpose. The government had not been able to assemble so many and such resolute policemen on that famous night in April, 1961, when the Premier, Michel Debré, went on the radio and tearfully implored the citizens—who had suddenly become worthy of consideration—to go on foot to the airport in Villacoublay, where they would stop the putschist mercenaries, who were allegedly flying in from Algiers to overthrow the "Republic," with a barrage of house slippers and holy water. But this was far more serious, and the powers that be showed their mettle. And as always when France asserts itself, this display of force embodied the wonderful magnanimity of the regime, an alliance of the rich and strong against the weak and poor. It was that solemn occasion, the day of the fall opening of the University of Paris. Ever since then, that day, which ought to be the one in which France's intellectual effulgence achieves its apotheosis in contemplative souls and in the radiance of knowledge, has become a day notable for its police attacks.

The champions of French culture saw a similar spectacle at the end of the same month, November, 1963, when the same students, in despair because lack of space in the auditoriums kept them from attending their lectures, decided to stage a demonstration at the same time that Mr. Segni, the President of Italy, would be visiting Paris. He was to receive—and did receive—an honorary doctorate at one of those interminable official masquerades which take up two-thirds of the time of government officials in regimes based on personal power. The chief of police started by forbidding the demonstration—probably because the Constitution guarantees the citizen's right to assemble—and warned the students that they would risk a sure six-month prison term if they persisted in demanding to be taught. The police struck again, with all the violence and hatred for the citizen that sets the French police apart from any other; and, going further than necessary to disperse the demonstrators, they unhesitatingly followed instructions, which were not merely to get traffic moving again but to get in a few licks of retributive justice for the government. That afternoon at the Odéon intersection, I watched as cheerful squads of police inspected the passers-by and, when they spotted young people in the crowd, leaped on them and treated them to a clubbing well after the demonstration had been broken up. As every schoolboy knows, *one has no possible recourse* against this sort of oppression. Let the victim protest and the court will condemn him for resisting an officer; let a passer-by remonstrate and he will be beaten up and carted off. As for the feeble protests of the press, they have long since ceased to have any effect either on those in power or on public opinion.

Dictatorship starts the moment that public opinion, dulled by propaganda, finds what is normal admirable, and what is loathsome normal. It was strange enough to see hordes of police banning the Latin Quarter to the very people who were supposed to be going back to school on opening day; it became stranger still, not to mention revelatory of the *nature* of the regime, to see a parade of students crushed like a formidable armed insurrection precisely when a foreign chief of state happened to be paying a visit, and a futile one at that. Why? Because the affair had touched the regime on a sensitive spot. Eighty percent of its activity being public relations, and one of its favorite impostures being to use the (undeserved) prestige of the Sorbonne to attract a foreigner here in order to trumpet our superiority by bestowing this signal honor upon him, the regime felt that it would be humiliated if this foreigner saw that the Sorbonne was designed more for ministerial show than for teaching.

One would like to know whether Mr. Segni, in his heart of hearts, was not more scandalized to learn that young men had been brutally clubbed in his name than he would have been to see a student fracas. His office and the circumstances did not permit him to reveal his disgust, but he did not attempt to hide it from his entourage on his return to Rome. Operation Prestige having thus been brought to a successful conclusion, the affair became once again a matter of internal French politics.

The argument that the authorities used to hammer this point home was that the students' complaints should under no circumstances have been aired while a foreign chief of state was visiting the capital. Now, as might be expected, this argument did not fail to carry weight with the Left and Center-Left. Several newspapers famous for their independence pronounced the demonstration to be in bad taste. A profoundly conservative reaction, for "What will they think abroad?" is the objection Rightists always raise when they want to sweep an internal problem under the carpet. I remember that during the strikes of the summer of 1953 there was a hotelkeeper, a great reader of *L'Aurore*,[11] who kept telling me all the time: "You know, when the foreigners here in the hotel read that, they laugh at us." They certainly must have had better things to laugh at than the comments that this worthy Frenchman regaled them with every morning, and it was utterly useless for me to explain to him that I for one could not nourish

[11] A right-wing Paris daily, *L'Aurore* was pro-*Pieds noirs* during the Algerian War and consistently anti-labor and anti-parliamentary.—*Translator's note.*

myself on France's prestige among foreigners. Three-quarters of the Fifth Republic's policies being based on vanity and official receptions (even a man who refuses to collaborate with you will tone down his dissent from the day you invite him to dinner), wasn't it natural, and good tactics, for the students to express their dissatisfaction on that particular day? Since virtually no day in France ends without the Chief of State's either receiving foreign dignitaries or traveling abroad himself, it is really difficult to know when to time a demonstration in order not to offend what the Left considers to be good taste.

The most extraordinary thing about these events was the degree to which public opinion and the press considered police brutality against a most respectable demonstration to be quite normal. The outrageousness of what had happened was not even noticed. Oh, people were surprised all right, but as if some *normal* aspect of political life was involved, as though, for example, a minister had refused to receive a delegation, or the demonstration had simply been "broken up," as I have seen them broken up in London—that is, broken up without breaking heads. The indifference of the people with whom I discussed the events of that day gave me an acute sense of the extent to which all democratic feeling has atrophied in France. The abuse of power was no longer felt to be abuse of power.[12]

[12] In *Le Monde* of February 12, 1965, I find the following:

"After the demonstrations which took place Friday night following a meeting organized by M. Tixier-Vignancour [France's most famous lawyer, who saved General Salan from the firing squad.—*Tr.*], 141 persons were arrested and held in police custody in the former asylum of Beaujon until late Saturday morning.

"Among them were people—foreigners mostly—who had gone to the Saint-Germain Cinema, had not taken part in the demonstration, but who were picked up in the raid as they were leaving the theatre, where they had just seen *Pour l'exemple.* . . .

"One of them, W. H. Pfaeffle, described his experiences that night:

"'Before I understood what was happening, a policeman had grabbed me and put me in a police van which held a number of young men of many different nationalities. Some were laughing and rough-housing; others were as astonished and bewildered as I was—like the three Ameri-

The same people were ready to maintain that the Fifth Republic is no oppressor and that our despot is really quite well-behaved, for all that people like this need to feel perfectly free is for the club and the knout to be used moderately by those in power, and for the government to engage in no repressive acts so long as there is nothing to repress. And finally, after having so effectively encouraged the students, the Leftist press could devote itself for months to surveys on "the depoliticalization of our youth," gravely analyzing why it was impossible to get young people to demonstrate—instead of why it was impossible to get them into classrooms.

A year later, on December 3, 1964, a meeting of three thousand students was held at the Student Union, again to expose the same inadequacies. The demonstration that was planned to take place after the meeting was forbidden. Starting in the early afternoon, thousands of policemen, Black Marias, motorcycles and ambulances jammed the Latin Quarter. The radio announced that the Chief of Police, M. Papon, like

---

can soldiers who couldn't speak a word of French and kept saying to one another, "Maybe they think we're drunk!" Finally someone explained that there had been a demonstration by the national opposition. Some were shouting, "Tixier to power!" while a British tourist, also arrested without explanation, kept lamenting ironically, "Paris by night!"

" 'The police wagon stopped half an hour later; we were unloaded, searched, questioned, then locked in cells until noon the next day, when we were released after another identity check. Later, we read in the papers that 141 demonstrators were arrested. The police did its duty.'

"M. Lucin Doyennette reported that he was held under similar circumstances until the next day even though he showed the policemen his ticket for the Saint-Germain Cinema. He added: 'There were about forty foreigners among us—all nationalities and all angry and protesting, and demanding that they be allowed to telephone their embassies. The police refused them this right on the pretext that there were no telephones in the police station. Anyway, I realized that more than two-thirds of the people arrested had nothing to do with the demonstration; many of them did not even know about it. Like myself, most were arrested as they were leaving a movie theatre; others told me that they had been taken into custody at the entrance to a café or subway, and that sometimes they had been treated with considerable brutality.'

"According to M. Michel David, who was also arrested at the en-

Clemenceau visiting the trenches in 1918, "was personally inspecting the security arrangements." The students decided not to demonstrate, probably recalling that the clubbings they had been treated to the year before had not even earned them a few columns of sympathy in the press. The day before, the vice president of the Student Union of France, M. Lévy, had been beaten up in the street by half a dozen Rightist goons, but at that particular moment no "guardian of the peace" had been around to protect him. Moreover, after the 1963 demonstration, the Minister of Education cut off the subsidy that he—that is, the citizens through the intermediary of the state —used to give to the Student Union, the organization which represents the majority of French students.[13]

The French are fussy about dictatorships. You have to have a Hitler, a Mussolini or a Franco at the head of the French state to merit the name. Mention the Gaullist dictatorship and they answer: "Excuse me, but where are the crematory ovens?"

We should not be so particular! We've been spoiled by Stalinism and Nazism. The Frenchman, who always tends to belittle himself, underestimates his own achievements. No sooner had de Gaulle returned as The Savior, through the good offices of that classic triptych of military defeat, financial

---

trance to the Saint-Germain Cinema, one of his fellow prisoners was a young man whose wife was sick and who 'had gone down to call a doctor, leaving her alone with a baby. He had been arrested before he had a chance to phone the doctor, and the police refused to call one for her. I witnessed his numerous requests to telephone all during the night, and each time he was refused with a snarl.'

"M. David also noticed that among those arrested were 'about a dozen North Africans who were insulted both by the demonstrators and by the police.'"

What good can mere condemnation do when the dignity of the citizen has been so trampled on in France that no one finds such incidents abnormal any more? It is useless to try to cover them up.

[13] To compensate, at the beginning of 1965, our press played up the repression of student demonstrations in Spain, and severely condemned the violence meted out to them and also to the students in Morocco.

crisis and anti-parliamentary nostalgia, than our Leftist friends gushed: "It's not Fascism." Compared to what? Let's discard the notion of Fascism and use democracy as a criterion. After all, if you complained that your apartment was too small, you wouldn't want someone to keep telling you that it was better than a coffin. The very fact that people go into ecstasies at any measure of our General-President that is remotely liberal proves that they judge him by a dictator's standards. You don't go around thanking the neighborhood butcher for not murdering you, or the friend whom you invite to dinner for not stealing your wallet. The only "real" Fascism France ever experienced was during the Occupation. The personal power of our kings and of Napoleon III admitted an opposition. And here we are, thrilling with pride because the regime, following the modern approach of putting students on the honor system, lets journalists censor their own writings; but we forget that at the end of the Second Empire the opposition press was of such virulence as to attain a circulation to which no opposition organ could aspire today without promptly dying of its own presumption. Bland editorial content, few readers. Cardinal rule: upset no habits. A rare elevation in tone, a markedly lower level in all else. Serious analyses, ludicrous circulation. Or take another tack: humor the public; try pompous journalism, *i.e.,* Gaullist or Gaulloid—for the Left doesn't feel that it can win readers on its own. It thinks that in order to seduce them it must wear heavy make-up, disguise itself. And because it is permitted to go out in broad daylight in this get-up, the Left swoons with gratitude at the feet of its benefactor. This is why you get the impression that the government itself has elicited whatever opposition manifests itself: for at times the opposition will support the government; at other times it will undertake the terrible task of criticism only after a great show of grief and guilt and protestations of love; and at still other times it will, in its gauche fashion, imitate the government.

Parliamentarism has been criticized from the viewpoint of

a "modern" conception of the state much more brilliantly than the plebiscitary state has been criticized from the viewpoint of a modern conception of democracy. One of the main arguments used against the parliamentary system, even in England, is that industrial societies pose problems that are increasingly of a technical nature. The average deputy, incapable of solving such problems, is inevitably reduced to representing only the small-town aspirations of his constituency. I will pass over the habitual gross exaggeration which has it that all past republican parliaments were peopled with perfect idiots, since this exaggeration is, in fact, the only original achievement of the Fifth Republic, the only idea that it has not stolen from its forerunners and taken personal credit for. Very well. But can anyone tell me what the present-day Frenchman, in this so-called direct democracy of ours, knows about these celebrated technical, economic, financial and diplomatic questions that do in fact shape his destiny? He is asked to choose personally the man to put in power, but never to approve or disapprove the way in which the power is used, the decisions that the man makes or proposes to make, the long- or short-term consequences, of which the French voter knows nothing, for *they are never explained to him.* If the government were to set up a referendum asking us to choose between a policy of austerity in favor of the nuclear deterrent, and a policy of housing, education, health and scientific research, clearly explaining that we would have to choose between one and the other and why, *then* one could talk about direct democracy. Such not being the case, we can only discuss a system that has been designed to keep one man and his entourage in power, in the name of hazy slogans like "grandeur and independence."

The results achieved under these slogans indicate the fact that the team in power has in seven years succeeded in making the French people the only literate people that no longer feels that it must understand in the slightest what the politicians for whom it is asked to vote intend to do when in power. It no longer even sees that the act of voting has anything to do with the difficulties that it encounters in daily life. If direct democracy means applauding individuals, and at the same time allowing yourself to be denied even the rudiments of news and opinion—information—about the most basic questions of life, both in the nation and in the world, then I will gladly concede that France is not at the moment under a dictatorship. Elections do not make democracy. The conditions—particularly those governing information—under which an election is held count for more than the election itself.

For the collective lobotomy that has been performed on us is an operation that can only take place under the anesthetic of chronic under-information. As everybody knows, fasting dulls the appetite. Likewise, the desire for knowledge cannot spring from ignorance. When news and opinion—information—fall below a certain level, it becomes impossible to arouse a nation's curiosity; the public can no longer "follow" things, just as a student who has missed several lessons cannot "follow" a blackboard demonstration of a mathematics problem. The average Frenchman, when viewing his present situation, does not know the real factors that caused it. The only ones who do know are those who keep informed because that is part of, indeed *is*, their job: *i.e.*, roughly speaking, the readers of *Le Monde*. But between *Le Monde* and France yawns an abyss so wide that no bridge can span it. What are three hundred thousand readers of *Le Monde* compared to thirty million Frenchmen at the age of reason who read their local papers, watch television and listen to the radio? True, the influence of *Le Monde* far surpasses its circulation, but this influence extends only to the upper echelons of society, not to the lower. The government knows that the French workers do not spend their time reading *Le Monde*, but watching television. The information in *Le Monde*, while often fatal to official doctrines, could under no circumstances give rise to an opposition viewpoint for its readers are individuals who separately feel certain intellectual needs but who could never join forces to produce a movement.

One of the many examples occurred at the end of 1964 when "Sirius"[14] ran an editorial in the issue of December 2 which demonstrated that the atomic bomb not only was useless from a military point of view, but also had produced no scientific advances to speak of and was upsetting our economy to boot. The article converted, whether they admitted it or not, all political groups, not to mention every French political figure, including the Premier and the Minister of the Armed Forces. But there was no possibility that the well-founded views of France's leading newspaper would have the least effect on either the government or the public. The development of the *force de frappe* was not halted, although all well-informed Frenchmen (a small number, admittedly) were opposed to it for irrefutable reasons; it was not halted because the government, which wanted the *force de frappe* for propaganda reasons, was supported by that vast number of uninformed Frenchmen—in other words, by the nation.

Under such circumstances, what point would there be in offering the masses a confutation? A confutation is nothing unless "counter-information" and "counter-opinion" are available. Now, counter-information reaches half a million people in France, not 52 million citizens (this time I included even new-born babies, since they're just about as well-informed as the adults).

Now, information is the bread of modern democracy. Any twentieth-century government that fails to keep its citizens informed is every bit as criminal as those governments in the past that let whole populations die of hunger. I am talking about information (news and opinion) for the *masses*, which is all that can be considered an advance, for there is nothing particularly modern about information for the elite: in France

[14] "Sirius" is the pseudonym of Hubert Beuve-Méry, editor-in-chief of *Le Monde.—Translator's note.*

one percent of the population has always known exactly what was going on and why. But this means nothing so long as the other ninety-nine percent do not. It is curious to note that the more people talk about the increasing complexity of the modern world—which forces the government to confide in an increasing number of technicians and Leftist editorialists—the less they realize that this very complexity argues for a large-scale diffusion of detailed information: in fact, it becomes *indispensable* if one is to keep the masses unceasingly informed of the real factors that affect their lives. If it can be done for commercial interests, why not for politics, economics, education and urban development? If it can be done with lies, why not with truth? Today a statesman who monopolizes for his *propaganda* the means of *information* that belong to the whole people is guilty of exactly what the civil servant who filches state funds is guilty of. The principle is the same. An anti-democratic instinct that is absolutely "primeval" (to use one of the intellectuals' favorite words) constrains all the intellectuals of the French Left—indeed, all Frenchmen—*to think that the more complex and serious our problems are, the fewer citizens are worthy of being informed about them.* As though it were really so difficult to explain what's going on in France and in the world in a way that everyone could understand!

Our elite groups exaggerate the amount of intelligence that graces their own cranial cavities. The sedulous scholars of the *Que sais-je* series[15] and the mimeo'd sheets at the Sciences-Po[16] are really quite ludicrous, with their air of being willing to pay for their high priestdoms in the existing order. Moreover, by virtue of a logical contradiction that is characteristic also of

---

[15] A series of popular monographs on the arts, literature, science, technology, religion, etc.—*Translator's note.*

[16] Detailed notes on the lecture courses given at the Institut des Sciences Politiques are in great demand at exam time. For the most part, the students who frequent the Sciences-Po are less serious than those who attend the specialized schools of the University of Paris.—*Translator's note.*

the Leftist French intellectual, they wax enthusiastic about mass media and the role of communication in society—at least to the degree that it enables them to obtain sinecures in alleged "research," which usually involves dressing up "mass communication" in the philosophic jargon that serves as the lingua franca of some two hundred Parisians. A famous writer recently said: "The real sign of freedom is shoes." Inasmuch as the average Frenchman possesses three pairs of shoes, we can be said to be very, very free. And in 1970 we will be freer still, since by then we will each probably have five pairs. In short, mass communication is a matter of new soles; freedom is available through the Maison André, the cobbler who knows how to cobble. But I, on the contrary, maintain that barefoot or shod, on stumps or on stilts, we had better learn that freedom is available through the Maison Philips.[17] We have to fight for it (for freedom, I mean, since the government is already fighting for Philips).

Though we are advised to begin building the Ideal Man from the nether extremities up—by virtue of which we must place in the vanguard of liberty those celebrated five-legged sheep[18] who for twenty years have been building socialism with one foot in the University, one in the Leftist press, one in the women's magazines, one in publishing and one in their family incomes—we beg leave to put it off for the moment: their television appeal is not yet what it should be.

It is normal for television to have become of prime importance in a regime that is founded essentially on public relations. Today the art of governing the French boils down to convincing them that all the good things that come their way are owing to the intelligence and benevolence of the govern-

[17] A popular make of radio and television sets.—*Translator's note.*
[18] "Mouton à cinq pattes" i.e., a prodigy, someone who achieves the impossible, an unlikely occurrence.—*Translator's note.*

75

ment, and all the bad things to the stupidity and malevolence of its enemies, both at home and abroad (hostility beginning where adulation ceases). Additionally, the art of governing employs the well-known advertising technique of fabricating an event (a press conference, perhaps; or the translation of Jean Moulin's ashes to the Pantheon) when nothing is really happening; and when something really important does happen, something that the government had no hand in or that it finds unpleasant (*e.g.*, scientific advances in other countries; unwanted strikes in France), then it insists that it is of no interest or even that it hasn't really happened. Television is the government's press agent just as the special correspondents who covered the Olympics in Japan in 1964 were not there to report the games but to act as press agent for the French contestants. Here's the sort of thing they were cabling home: "Two French runners came in eighth and fifteenth respectively," or "A Frenchman almost won in such and such an event."

When a foreigner won, you could figure out who it was only with the greatest difficulty and after a long and arduous process of deduction. The most way-out specialties—pedal craft, hopping and creeping on your back—were the objects of unusual commentaries because there was some French competitor who had a chance of winning. One relic of old, tandem-bike racing, was played up in advance, probably because our journalists thought that the vehicle on which the proletariat of the Popular Front had ridden to the conquest of leisure time and paid vacations would, with such a head start, twenty-eight years later forge gloriously ahead "to lead the field of nations of the entire world." But, alas, our two cyclists lost, and we were treated to lengthy and learned disquisitions on why they failed. One thesis that was elaborated consisted in a technical explanation, and it was presented as being quite extraordinary and of the highest degree of interest: namely,

that our cyclists had not managed to synchronize the move-
ments of their legs and, given the nature of the tandem bicy-
cle, this could indeed be considered a flaw in their performance. I cite this feat of rhetoric, wafted to us by the French
Radio-Television Network, because it is exactly the kind of
owlish and superfluous explanation that the government gives
when something goes wrong in politics or economics.

The chief characteristic of regimes based on personality is
that they must fabricate events without let-up, strive constantly to catch the public eye with theatrical tricks, which
grow the more elaborate the less they have to do with politics
or, when the events *are* political, they are the kind which the
public cannot understand and of which it remembers only the
theatrical aspect. Under democratic regimes, the importance
of an event determines the amount of information devoted to
it; in a modern dictatorship, the amount of information sup-
plied determines the importance of the event. Without this
information and especially without television, which by substituting a picture for an idea disguises the nonexistence of the
fact, the event would not exist. It exists by virtue of its having
been televised. A wedding trip is only a wedding trip if you
see it: the stating of it is of no interest and makes its news
value nil. But although substituting the image for the an-
nouncement gives the event its own visual reality, though the
event may be one in an already familiar series of thousands, it
cannot confer, in the political sphere, any additional richness
of content. That is why the use of images, which in any case is
centered entirely on official circles, aims to cover reality with
a shell of non-events. For example, on December 19, 1964,
everyone thought it was wonderful that the President stood in
the cold, clad in a simple military uniform and without a coat,
while he listened to André Malraux deliver a speech on Jean
Moulin at the Pantheon. But this non-event became an event
only because it was televised. The respect due to the memory

of Jean Moulin was hardly grounds for risking a presidential cold. This sort of valor doesn't do anyone any good. An intelligent nation would have preferred Malraux's speech to have been more understated and the General's dress less so. We are approaching a stage of civilization in which the French, who have become incapable of following the drift of political speeches, will react only to the physical surroundings of the orator, who will have to make his speeches while leaning over the edge of a precipice in order to be sure of winning their enthusiastic votes.

In France, television and the "audio-visual media" in general, have been the object of intense curiosity for the past five or six years—a curiosity that is both childish and snobbish, like that which motorists of 1900 had for their cars. The audio-visual media do not yet appear to be taken for granted, like running water or the telephone; we are still surprised that they exist at all. Most of the public has no criteria by which it can judge French television. What strikes them most is the miracle of having private movies right in their own homes; what the program is doesn't matter, for the choice is between the official offering and nothing at all. It's exactly what would happen in a country where there had never been a press, and where one day the state created a single newspaper, which it then proceeded to control. Even if everyone read the paper, could you honestly maintain that the people of this country knew what modern journalism really was? Obviously they would not know its virtues or its faults, its greatness or its shame.

The French television public is now at the stage that small-town audiences once were in relation to the cinema: no matter what, they would go to see the weekly feature at the lone moviehouse. Sometimes they left the hall happier than at other times, but they were never completely dissatisfied, for the quality of the film counted less than the pleasure of seeing pictures move. But as soon as one can make comparisons one's attitude changes. The technical achievement as such, the miracle of long-distance vision, is no longer all that excites one. This has already happened with the radio: when our listeners were able to compare the boring, censured, stuttering news bulletins of the official station with the brilliant, meaty, intelligent reporting of the so-called "peripheral" stations—which were honest to boot, until the French government bought controlling interest in them—they stopped listening to the state radio almost entirely. And today, as during the Algerian War, or when there is a foreign or domestic crisis or any international event, good or bad, insignificant but talked about, or important but slighted—no one, worker or professional journalist, peasant or diplomat, supporters or non-supporters of those in power, no one, absolutely no one, would dream of listening to a news bulletin on one of the state radio stations. When you say you are "listening to the news," you mean you are listening to Radio Europe or Radio Luxemburg. And if one or both of these stations falls into line with the official stations, then you just don't listen to anything at all, because you know better.

Television, then, is still at the stage where it exists, but is nothing to brag about, just as a local newspaper exists but is nothing to brag about. This is what makes the reactions to television of critics, journalists and writers all the more astonishing. Intellectuals are so afraid that they will be accused of slighting this new means of communication through devotion to an older form of culture that they demonstrate an unwonted vehemence when they laud or revile the products for the home screen. Let me make myself clear: I have no quarrel with those who study the psycho-sociology of television and its viewers; I am talking about the reactions of intellectuals as viewers. Their desire not to be behind the times leads them into a kind of demagogy with regard to this audio-visual medium. Whether they praise or blame, they show such a burning interest in whatever idiocy the sacred studios turn out, that one is reminded of the comportment of courtiers who feel threatened by a new master. It is highly instructive to stop watching television for a year but to go on reading television reviews in the papers. After a month of it, you start to feel that television really does exist after all. The program that you don't see but read about in the reviews begins to take on a personality; praise and condemnation combine to make you feel that it is indeed something worth talking about. After three months, even unfavorable criticism of the news program seems, paradoxically, to inflate its importance: for no matter how harsh the criticism may be, it is flattering in the sense that it treats the program as though it were a genuine televised newspaper. The only trouble is that the poor news announcer hasn't even attained that level of being that permits him to have strengths and weaknesses. As for the really big programs, those which are on the air once a month, they are announced, followed and criticized in tones suitable to the first performance of *Le Sacre du printemps*, the world première of *The Gold Rush* or the Armory Show. After a year of such reading, you picture an extraordinarily warm and animated world, where the best exists along with the worst, but where everything is bathed in a most stimulating vitality. Now turn on the TV set and take a good look. Your first sensation—apart from any evaluation of the programs themselves, whether they are good, bad or indifferent—will be of a general loss of tension. For the old man who is confined to an armchair and does nothing but watch the street from his window, the most trifling neighborhood event is far more important than the rest of the world. When you go from the reviews to television itself, from commentaries to the reality commented on, you suddenly realize that this reality is vastly overrated.

First, it is overrated quantitatively: only a few hours each day are given over to the transmission of programs. The bedridden, who depend on television to distract them, know this well. Forty-five minutes during the day and three hours at night—such, not counting educational and regional programs, is the weekday allowance. On weekends and holidays, religion and sports are recruited to fill the gaps. Compared to the thirteen American channels, which broadcast continuously every day from seven in the morning until two or even five A.M., to the seven or eight Japanese channels and, in Europe, to the systems of Germany and England, French television is still in the embryonic stage. And since the sociologists of "mass communication" are so receptive to quantity, I would like to point out that nobody worries about traffic problems in countries that have only one car for every ten thousand inhabitants. And if this car attracts crowds of passers-by, perhaps it is only because they haven't yet got used to motor vehicles.

Secondly, television is overrated qualitatively. If it were really what it's supposed to be and what it seems to be when you read the television columns in the press, then important programs like *Cinq colonnes à la une* would be the kind of news program that we would get daily. As for the regular news broadcasts, they are an insult to the viewer; it's as though a school had one instructor to teach a compulsory course and, instead of giving a history or biology lesson, all he did was describe his daily routine in detail, from breakfast to brushing his teeth at night, garnishing the whole with a few banal stories, and then at exam time demanded a complete mastery of his monologues. During every two- or three-month period, a good half of the news program is devoted to official ceremonies showing governmental dignitaries greeting their guests or hosts (as the case may be): the emphasis is entirely on protocol—arrival at the airport, entering the Hall of Honor, speeches, flowers, cars swooshing away, handshakes on the Elysée lawn, lines of cops and gala evenings—all those tired images that used to lend their soporific charms to movie newsreels and to which everyone long ago awarded the grand prize for boredom, *ex aequo* with certain "documentaries"; and this pandering to public relations to which French officialdom is committed does not, it goes without saying, suggest any analysis of the possible political importance of so much distressing pomposity.

Once again I ask what sort of regime we are living under when—no matter what is happening in the rest of the world and with complete disregard for the natural order of importance—the main event of the day on television is always a speech or trip of the Chief of State or one of his associates? And as for political debates, all we get is . . . an interview with the cabinet minister who has jurisdiction over the national and international ramifications of the subject under discussion! That's right. We have fallen so low that we are not even shocked when the announcer fervently tells us that this evening we will be privileged to have a "debate" on European agriculture (or housing or education) and that the "debate" will consist of an interview: so-and-so from the French Radio-Television Network will be questioning the minister concerned. This format, moreover, represents an extreme in anarchic license, for usually it is only the minister who says anything—it's so much safer that way. Needless to say, they would never think of inviting someone to offer a solid rebuttal.

Several years ago, when I was in London in the middle of a transport strike, I watched the Minister of Labor take part in a debate, or rather in two debates (one on BBC and the other on a commercial channel) in which the union officials argued with him on a footing of complete equality. The minister did not necessarily have the upper hand; far from it; nothing was rigged in advance. The labor unions clearly would not have stood for it; and as for the minister, he could not have refused to debate without admitting defeat in the public eye, since he had been publicly invited by the two channels. That day I saw that television (and radio, for it, too, can perform the same service) can play a really important role in a democracy; and I saw very vividly what "direct democracy," which we French hear so much about and are led to believe is essentially a soliloquy by the President of the Republic, can really be in a democratic country. True, speeches given in the National Assembly are sometimes shown on television, but this is another hoax, for the coverage is usually biased, and the anti-government man is reduced to a couple of sentences, chosen for preference from among those in which he stumbles, after which the minister involved (or the prime minister) rises like a vengeful god, high-minded, urbane and omnipotent, and naturally has the last word—and everyone knows that under the Fifth Republic a minister's last word is good for fifteen minutes of program time. And in the face of all this, our propaganda chief dares to affirm that our radio and television news broadcasts are subject to no pressure from the powers that be! Sometimes he even takes it into his head to scoff at the freedom that supposedly reigns in British television. What is astonishing is not that he should say what he says, but that the public should, without even raising an eyebrow, accept these remarks, which could be uttered only in a country in which the citizenry has forgotten that a certain consideration is due them.

For some time there has been a good deal of talk about permitting advertising on television. Paradoxically, the most sensible position for the Left to take would be to fight not against television advertising (which is inevitable, for too much money is involved), but for the creation of separate commercial channels to be financed entirely by advertising. In the present French situation, we must join forces with the moneyed interests in order to break the monopoly on radio and television news, which, given the anti-democratic ways of the French, no regime could resist employing in a dishonest fashion. If we end up with commercial advertising on state-controlled television, if we have to put up with commercials *and* pay the radio-TV tax, this would be—*will* be—that synthesis of all possible disadvantages which France possesses the secret of bringing about. Then we will have, in the sphere of information as in everything else, all the faults of capitalism and none of its advantages.

Once the lion's share has been taken by official governmental ceremonies, by those non-events that the regime exudes in order to call attention ceaselessly to itself and distract attention from its policies, and by the propaganda of the Chief of State or his assistants, the newscast suddenly tapers off during the few remaining minutes or seconds into dateless human interest stories: dog shows, geranium expositions, suburban mishaps. The latter, intended to be cute, are told with heavy-handed humor, emphasized by a pallid smile from the announcer, who seems unaccustomed to smiling but who determinedly tells himself that it's time for a little comic relief. For the main thing you notice about French television is the paucity of pictures: listening to someone deliver a monologue is often boring and irritating, but watching him is absolutely unbearable, especially—and this is true of nine-tenths of our television newscasters—when the speaker lacks naturalness, ease and the precise diction which make an audience enjoy watching and hearing him. Instead, we get affected gestures, stiffness, butchered words followed by clumsy excuses, grating voices—everything that could possibly torture the viewer.

Another curse of newscasts is the mania for over-naming: "What's going on, Louis-Georges Dubourg?" "What is the political situation on Oran, Jacques Frostier?" "Thank you, Robert Dupont-Boissart." But that, you will reply, is like signing your name to a written article. In point of fact the comparison is not valid: newscasts are made with *time*. The reason that commercials shown at the movies are so irritating is that they are forced on you within the time that you have purchased, but printed advertisements do not get in the way of the articles in a paper. Very well, newscasting has become a mixture of government propaganda and pointless little stories;

but the sacrifice of our dignity as citizens should at least have earned us the pleasure of seeing a performance competently done by agreeable humorists. If I understand aright, the recent theories of my fellow philosophers on "the specificity of the televisual phenomenon," television's job is to tell something in pictures, to make you *see*. Now, all I ever see are events that take place close to home, on the Elysée lawn or at Orly, and which I could easily see firsthand if I weren't so anxious not to. And what do I see? I see a man who is as embarrassed as a theatre director who has to go out on stage to tell a booing audience that the performance will not take place. This journalist reads from several sheets of paper on which are described, with the most brilliant feeling for logical order and transitions, a fire in New Zealand, a landslide in Luxemburg (here his voice becomes serious and his eyelids drop: profound sympathy), the collapse of a church in a small village in Mexico, police helicopters flying over Limoges during the cold snap, heaps of gifts around London bobbies at Christmastime (every year), the accidental discovery by bulldozer either of a mine left over from the last war or of Gallo-Roman bones (musical accompaniment: Saint-Saëns' *Danse macabre*), etc.

As for the "Last Minute News" broadcast, while it does come at the last minute of the program, it is not really up to the minute, for it is generally devoted to some event which has been in the papers since the evening before. In short, the newscast resembles a provincial newspaper. It is made up of the same things that you find in *Le Comtois, La Voix du Nord* and *Ouest-France:* political conformity and human interest stories—worthy mothers ("our heartiest congratulations to Mrs. X"), a local peasant who fell off his motorbike, neither man nor bike sustaining the least damage but both photographed and reproduced in the paper above the caption "A Close Call." Whenever there is a strike or demonstration, French Radio-Television always shares the resigned indignation of the main victim of such events, which, as everyone knows, is the "worker," who was peacefully going "to *work*" or "home from *work*." In this way a pointless story is linked to propaganda. On April 14, 1962, French Radio-Television glorified Prime Minister Pompidou: "Once upon a time there was a little boy named Georges Pompidou . . ." We see here the first appearance in France of the American myth that "anyone can become President of the United States," *but applied to an appointive office at the disposal of the ruler.* Instead of the log cabin, where Lincoln's grandparents died under Indian arrows, we see the Doric columns of the Rothschild Bank and a scalp dance in Auvergne,[19] and instead of an election by a great people a selection by a tall man.[20]

What are we to conclude of the intellectual level and degree of political independence of a people that thinks reading provincial French papers and watching news broadcasts on television will keep it abreast of what is going on at home and abroad? One has to read the English papers in order to get any idea of where French events fit in the international scale of importance—to find out, for instance, that de Gaulle's trip to Latin America in 1964 did not get detailed coverage by the

[19] Pompidou was General Director of the Rothschild Bank from 1956 to 1962 and was on the Commission on Tourism from 1946 to 1949.—*Translator's note.*
[20] On June 1, 1960, *Le Monde* summed up an article on French television in *The Times* of London as follows:

"'Chaotic experiments involving numerous programs which appear and disappear with astonishing rapidity' was the chief impression of *The Times*' Paris correspondent. But the writer does not offer criticism alone. He points out that, even though it is aimed at an elite, French television is watched by all segments of the population and 'helps spread cultural values in a country where, in any case, they have never been the privilege of any one class.' However, even though he praises *Lectures pour tous* and *Magazine des arts,* he thinks that there are too many serious professorial faces on our television screens. 'It is an honorable thing to seek to spread culture,' he writes, 'but one wonders if it is necessary to do it in so irritatingly didactic a way.' And he deplores the fact that so few playwrights have decided to write especially for television.

"*The Times* article centers its criticism on the handling of the news.

world press because it had little practical significance and because public relations trips have no moral significance whatsoever. By dint of reading six or seven Parisian papers, one can nonetheless get a rough idea of what is going on inside France, provided one is also familiar with the use of allusion, periphrasis and circumlocution, and provided one knows that when such and such a newspaper says thus and so, the alert reader must, on the basis of a certain pattern, interpret the statement as meaning something else, which is not clearly stated. What we call an opposition newspaper is just antagonistic enough to displease the government without really inconveniencing it; just favorable enough to appear to be only temporarily and accidentally pro-government; just critical enough to make one reflect without making one change one's mind; and just alarmist enough so that condemnation of the past is only a preamble to announce an imminent solution. In France, being well-informed requires a considerable labor of acquisition of data,

---

It notes that 'the paternalistic influence of the government, to say nothing of the vigilance of the Church, tends to result in programs that are more instructive than interesting.' The writer remarks that no one could say that French television is politically controlled, because, he adds, 'no such control is necessary. Everyone knows exactly how far he can go.' And *The Times* continues: 'This self-censorship makes official censorship very rare. But it makes the ninety-five minutes of news dreadfully dull.'

"As an example, he recalls that when the Algerian National Liberation Front suggested that Ben Bella open negotiations with France, the only thing on television was General de Gaulle's trip to Alsace and that the next day there was not even the slightest allusion to the N.L.F.'s proposal.

"*The Times* continues: 'The new press chief has said that he considered this program to be entertainment, not a news service. . . . In that case it is entertainment seen entirely through rose-colored glasses and without the slightest trace of unpleasant reality.'

"Only *Cinq colonnes à la une* gives one any idea of what a lively, stimulating news program could be. 'It is significant,' writes *The Times*, 'that this controversial ninety-minute program goes on only once a month.'

"Apparently *The Times* has few illusions concerning the reactions of the French public: 'Any influence that can be exercised will not come from the bottom but from the top. In France, the absence of political discussion on television is more often accepted than condemned.' "

comparison and interpretation: it is not a right but a profession, a specialty, sometimes even larceny.

There exists, then, in France a *de facto* censorship that is much more effective than official censorship, and it increases every year as the very lack of information destroys the desire for information. The censorship is both political and moral: a program entitled "Close-up of Salvador Dali" was suppressed because the artist mentioned homosexuality and onanism; in 1964 a program dedicated to the cartoonist Robert Siné, well-known for his opposition to Church and Crown, was canceled at the last minute. There is also personal revenge, as when in 1959 Robert Hirsch of the Comédie-Française was punished because, according to an official memorandum, he was guilty "of having been unthinkably offensive with regard to his own guardian minister [of culture, André Malraux] in a broadcast on April 13." The memorandum goes on to say that the actor will not be allowed to take part in any future radio or television broadcasts and that his name should not even be mentioned on the air.

Such occurrences are so frequent that the French no longer even notice them. Abuse of power does not seem to discredit the regime, since whatever filters through the curtain of censorship and sees the light of day is held up as a proof of how liberal the government really is. The fact that someone like Jean Nocher, an odious troublemaker whose only interest in life is to spit on everything that is fine and noble, can spout off evening after evening and year after year on Paris-Inter, that is, on the only official radio station that can be heard everywhere in the country, that he is permitted to disseminate the virus of French mediocrity and sow his Right-wing, petit-bourgeois seeds that are capable of destroying all humanity, just for his own vanity and personal interest—the fact, I repeat, that this man should be tolerated doesn't strike anyone as strange, even though he is one of the few who are allowed to speak "unrehearsed" (which is what his program is called), *i.e.*, without supervision. And on what program or station do we find the counterblast to this rot? For, since French Radio-Television, which is a monopoly, does not recognize the right of reply, none of Nocher's victims—starting with the principal one, the nation which he disgraces—has ever been allowed to have his say at the same hour and on the same station. Everybody knows all this: people laugh and joke about it, say that it's a disgrace—but they put up with it and, worse still, don't really get upset about it. Even the fact that François Mauriac's servile puff of de Gaulle is the subject of endless radio broadcasts leads them to no conclusions about the nature of the regime.

"The writer," we read in *Le Monde*, "discussed his book on de Gaulle with Jacques Paoli on Europe I and, *at greater length with Pierre de Boisdeffre during four 'interviews' broadcast over France-Inter by French Radio-Television, which did Mauriac the honor of granting him as well three interviews on television.* Apropos of these interviews, we note the curious participation of M. de Boisdeffre, the Director of Radio Broadcasting, who took the role of interviewer and, like a press attaché, bent over backwards to praise Mauriac's panegyric: we heard a conventional, well-tempered duet, cut and dried at best—not a real interview in the sense of a give and take of ideas." But everyone knows all that—people will tell you—and everyone except a few fanatics deplores it; there are even newspapers that make fun of it. First of all, what newspapers? Not the ones that the great French public reads.

As for the other papers, their ridicule strikes me as hardly appropriate and, what's more, hardly in keeping with that "nonpartisan" tolerance of theirs as they strive to treat the regime fairly, that is, solemnly count the number of times that the members of the opposition have been allowed to sneeze as so many blessings. Once again, it all depends on the way you look at it: if your ideal is a democracy worthy of a mature people, then you think things are eighty percent worse than they were; but if you are comparing the situation with an unenlightened despotism based on demagogy, then you consider the remaining ten percent of approximate freedom of information to be a gift of the gods. The powers that be also have their way of mocking the citizenry, and that is to affirm periodically that the information on radio and television is uncensored, that the government never brings any pressure to bear on the audio-visual media. They even prepare, announce and apply mysterious "directives" which are supposed to inject freedom into the monopoly, but after they are applied the television newscast gets still duller, still more "official" and still emptier. And the French can no longer even understand or feel that those in power are holding them in ever greater contempt, giving them one more slap in the face.

Mass communications have given rise to a combination of under- and over-information: under-information if something is important, over-information if it is pointless. In July, 1962, thanks to the artificial satellite Telestar, the first televised picture was beamed from France to the United States—a close-up of the cabaret singer Michèle Arnaud. . . . The choice illustrates an aspect of our present civilization: the more we transmit, the less attentive we are to the significance of what we transmit. Many naïvely believe that using audio-visual techniques by itself transforms the substance and value of what they convey, somewhat as, in the early days of mass newspapers, the mere fact that something was printed masked (and still does for most people) the stupidity or inaccuracy of what it was that appeared "in the papers." Another facet of over-information is the plethora of "interviews with writers and artists," which are beginning to take the place of knowledge of the works themselves. This practice has come about because setting up interviews with actors, film directors and writers is one of the easiest ways to fill up radio and television time.

Such interviews may add something to the understanding of fully realized works; but the tone they adopt—the "sublime, enigmatic and tender aspects of my creative talent" tone of these overnight idols and young film directors, just barely kept afloat thanks to a tiny following of Parisian snobs—inevitably makes you doubt their talent. For a real talent at the height of its creative vigor expresses itself in the work; and it must be disgusting to duplicate the new-born work by so tangential an approach as a commentary on oneself or, to be more accurate, as a complacent reconstruction of oneself in such a way that one will be considered a "visionary" in whom are to be discovered both incredibly complex designs and inexplicably fleeting impulses. Here too, in culture as in politics, in over- as in under-information, the communication is a mere sham; it keeps people away from what it claims to offer them and, while giving them the illusion of penetrating deeper and deeper into the secret of men and things, it leads them away. In reality, it is just as difficult to worm a bit of truth out of someone else as it is to write it yourself, and those who can do it in front of a camera or a microphone could also do it by themselves. The audio-visual medium cannot accomplish a miracle by itself, but it has the drawback of dulling the public's standards and critical sense, so that it thinks that it is being better nourished than ever, when in reality it is being fed pills to cut down the appetite. And as for the social groups that are experiencing mass communication for the first time thanks to television, they are being hoaxed as cruelly as would have been the first working-class children admitted in the elementary schools if they had been given deliberately falsified arithmetic books.

Politics and culture are both isolated from the people, both "in exile," as I said in my generalization at the beginning of this volume. The use to which radio and television are put in the cultural area must perforce resemble its use in the political. An old reactionary myth has it that if the masses only leave the worries of government to an authoritarian and omnipotent state, they will be free to concentrate peacefully on gardening and music. Being a docile, uninquisitive miner leads one more surely to an appreciation of the fine arts than does the perplexed state of mind of demanding, adult individuals, with whom our collective self is supposedly already overpopulated; the leisure time gained by giving up politics would encourage the masses to participate in the cultural life of their civilization. But despotism seems to have got along with art only in small cities or in great states whose intellectual life was modeled exactly on that of small cities: that is, only where intellectual life excluded the masses. The situation is quite different in a modern country, where everyone has finished elementary school at least and where every problem, no matter how far removed from politics it may seem, is nonetheless political in the sense that it concerns the life of the entire community. Everything is known immediately (under what form is another question: for most people, a writer is nothing but a series of echoes in the weeklies), and everything takes on meaning in relation to the whole of the national life. A literary prize, the television program for Christmas Eve, the authorization or banning of a film, the seizure of books that do not conform to certain standards of decency or that offer insufficient homage to the supreme chief, and particularly the reaction of public opinion—shaped by the audio-visual media of the state and nourished on predigested, presweetened culture (subtly censored without the public's knowledge)—these things have on instantaneous impact on the community. Culture has never been so little a matter of individual choice as it is today.

Anything which can be consumed by the individual in France today has been surreptitiously modeled by politicians for whom culture is a sort of warm bath that relaxes the public for the periodic civic capitulation of the plebiscites; to the politician, culture is a theme for propaganda that glorifies the possessors of power. In short, the modern state has decided to give the people more and more culture but less and less cultural freedom. Between the *"Maisons de la culture"* which, under the direction of the Minister of Cultural Affairs, are diffusing a perfectly harmless avant-garde throughout the provinces, and the disastrous radio and television programs which have accustomed it to an intellectual activity on a par with that of a society patroness, the French people have become anesthetized by habits which amount to a training in apathy. It is not accurate, therefore, to say that indifference to politics encourages culture, for public indifference to politics does not occur spontaneously; it is the fruit of intense activity on the part of the state, and a complex system which consumes a tremendous amount of energy is required to maintain it. And the state cannot afford to let the forces that politics do not absorb be channeled into culture, for they would immediately inundate politics. This is the reason that education is vegetating and that our press, radio, television and literary reviews emit an aura of respectability, scholastic obscurity and pretentious boredom which so impress foreigners when they have the misfortune to come in contact with us. In fact, in the life of the mind as well as in political life, it matters little that a product is dull or banal, *for it is not meant to be consumed.* What is meant to be consumed is the publicity that surrounds it.

It matters little that a product is great or moving; its function is still to serve as a springboard for propaganda. "In 1957," cried the Minister of Cultural Affairs in his speech to the National Assembly on the 1965 budget, "six hundred thousand people saw French paintings displayed abroad. This year, there were seven million of them. It may be a pity that the Venus de Milo was sent to Tokyo, but it was worth at least as much to us as a diamond-studded medal, for four million

Japanese saw the French flag behind that statue." Everything about this statement is striking: the innocence with which the minister confers French citizenship on a Greek work (he had already naturalized the Mona Lisa when he sent it to be exhibited in the United States); the allusion to the Olympic medals, intended to assuage our amour-propre but at the same time betraying the highly totalitarian view that art is some kind of "international competition"; the tendency to confuse French paintings *seen* abroad with French paintings *sent* abroad; and finally the purely quantitative evaluation of the life of the mind that permits him to parry other questions—like why there has not been a single large exhibit with a serious approach and *real* international prestige (since they insist on it) for the last five years (the last being the Poussin exhibit in 1960, which had been prepared long before under the Fourth Republic); why there is still no large exhibition hall in Paris to replace the Orangerie, which, having proved inadequate, is closed pending its being put to another use; or why, out of the comparatively few French paintings we have left, so many have been permitted to leave the country—not, this time, to be exhibited abroad temporarily, but to be sold (Georges de la Tour, Cézanne and most of the Bonnard legacy).[21] Malraux's speech on the Acropolis inaugurating the Philips *son et lumière* equipment, the highhanded appropriation of poor Braque's corpse, at the interment of which his whole work became one of the fruits of the Fifth Republic (though only an appallingly small number of his canvases could be collected for the subsequent exposition at the Louvre)—all this could be defended on the grounds that it is just part of the job. But in

[21] As for the large exhibitions, all those that we have seen after the Poussin Exposition have been traveling shows that stopped in Paris after touring other countries (*e.g.*, Coptic art and Mirò), or expositions of local interest, making use solely of the resources of our national museums. These exhibits were interesting enough, but no other nation in the world would dream of touting them as stupendous titles to fame.

my opinion such an excuse is erroneous, for it derives from an archaic conception of the state that I see no reason to perpetuate.

Moreover, we are not dealing with the duties of the job or with sidelines, but with the very principle of the cultural activities of the regime. In fact, if the regime speaks in astronomical figures when it comes to exploiting the Venus de Milo as a catalyst for the Japanese people, it substitutes rhetoric for figures when it comes to the cultural budget in France. I quote from *Le Monde* of November 12, 1963: "Interrupting dry arguments for a regrettably brief moment, the Minister of State prefaced the reading of his budget estimates with a dazzling definition of culture, a breath-taking paeon that left his audience enthralled. It was easy to forget that the figures which inspired this amazing demonstration *represented only 0.3 percent of the total State budget.*"

That was the budget estimate for 1964. One year later, at the presentation of the budget for 1965, we saw the same ministerial ecstasies (in which the Venus de Milo and the Japanese figured largely); but *Le Monde* (November 10) carried this simple headline: "Cultural affairs: budget virtually unchanged from 1964." This probably explains why admission fees to museums (those in England and the United States charge nothing) increase every year. Time was when man's thought manifested itself through literature, science, painting, philosophy, architecture. Now you just lump them together and call them "culture," as though this vague entity possessed an independent existence. From various expressions of thought, we have fallen into "culture." It remained for France to reduce culture to "Cultural Affairs."

But when one discusses the government's cultural policies with an ex-progressive turned sheepish Gaullist, his reflex actions are the same as they were when he used to discuss the Algerian War: everything good is owing to the well-defined will of one man, everything bad to unconquerable adversity. Just as a mother interprets every stammer of her little boy as a sign of genius, for the Gaullist the very existence of the Louvre is cause for wonder and daily thanks to the politicians whom he considers responsible for it, much as the ancient Mexicans believed that their gods were responsible for the rising of the sun and the return of the seasons, for they thought that the sun was recreated each day by a new decree of the celestial powers. Since the gods owe us nothing, zero is normal and anything more than that is a miracle. Or, to be more exact, the gods are doing us a favor if they refrain from using their powers to hurt us. This attitude has got such a hold on today's Frenchman, so accustomed is he to thinking that the subprefect who attends the opening of an agricultural exposition does so through sheer magnanimity that he no longer even thinks of judging a policy by comparing its potential with its results. For example, everyone knows that one of the favorite themes of government propaganda is the economic boom.

Now the French, including the Left, cannot keep from measuring the country's economic situation according to the standards of the poverty-stricken postwar period. They simply cannot make up their minds to judge France in accordance with the standards of the so-called affluent societies of North America and Western Europe, to compare their levels of production and consumption with those of the group of nations to which France belongs. City workers are always ready to go on strike or to stage demonstrations in order to obtain wage increases; peasants barricade highways and refuse to sell their milk for a period of time, but neither group manages to give a political expression to their difficulties at election time. And who would teach them? Aren't the leaders, so-called, of the Left the first to condemn the strikes and demonstrations for their old-fashioned subsistence demands? Aren't these leaders secretly intrigued by the regime's fake planning, and more inclined to praise the government's intentions and hobnob with its members than evaluate its results? If the people's protests are old-fashioned, whose job was it to have directed them toward the future? And in a republic where all the normal and legal channels of communication between the state power and the citizens have been suppressed, how are the demands to be aired? Or rather, might one not say that they are condemned to be *aired*, since there is no way to *express* them? One cannot hope to renovate a political climate unless one possesses some idea of the forces that motivate a people, a bit of imagination and the capacity to experience and arouse new emotions. At least that is the way it has always been. But today all that the Left does is attack the underpaid worker and his grievances, accusing him of Poujadism[22] and failure to understand the Plan.

When one examines the economic record of the Fifth Republic, it is not so much the record itself that seems original as the manner in which the state has advocated it and the opposition received it. Aggressive propaganda from the state; awe and pathological fright from the opposition. In keeping with their usual tactics, the powers that be described our economic development without any reference to the immediate past (except when they had to explain deficits) or to foreign points of reference. Our prosperity is thus explained as having begun in 1958 and not in 1952; the ideas and organs that the Fourth Republic invented are shamelessly appropriated and all setbacks are attributed to it, even seven years after its death. Compared to the United States, Japan, Germany, England,

[22] Pierre Poujade's movement started in 1953, initially as a protest by shopkeepers against discriminatory and "inquisitorial" taxes. By 1956 Poujadism was able to count two and a half million votes and fifty-two deputies. At the same time it was beginning to show all the signs of an embryonic Fascist movement: anti-parliamentarism, racism and colonialism. Today it is no longer a force to be reckoned with.—*Translator's note.*

Italy and the Scandinavian countries, we stand somewhere around the middle of the scale as far as annual growth rate and average per capita income go. Not an outstanding performance.

On the other hand, on such other essential issues as city planning, educational needs, the telephone, the distribution of national income and equitable taxation, the Fifth Republic's accomplishments have been nil. We lag farther behind than ever; inequalities are more pronounced than ever. Official propaganda has so skillfully cast a spell about the idea of abundance that no one would ever dream of questioning how the abundance is distributed. Naturally, the Left is the first to be bewitched, forgetting that in an industrial society abundance by itself is neither a miracle nor even a virtue, and that what counts is to know how it is produced and how it is distributed. For example, if a large part of the national income derives from real estate speculation, which the state has decided not to combat (and which, moreover, pretty well nips in the bud all the city planning and urban development projects of the official planners), and if in addition such income is rarely subject to taxation, it is hardly surprising that the result is inflation.

And if, in order to stop inflation, the state introduces a so-called "stabilization" plan which strikes principally at the buying power of the *wage earners*—that is, of that part of the national income which, as everyone knows, can be measured by income tax returns and which does not profit by speculation—then it is making labor pay for a crisis caused by speculation, without curbing speculation itself and without really stabilizing prices either. One cannot deny that the 1958 stabilization of the economy and the franc, the effort to achieve a balanced budget and equilibrium in the balance of payments and the 1963 struggle to stop inflation are admirable in principle—even if the results have been exaggerated and even though they are accompanied by chauvinistic affronts to other nations and, on the home front, by the demagogic use of slogans designed to trick the ignorant.[23] But who has ever maintained that capitalism has no interest in forging the instruments that will make it prosper? Will we, dazzled by the intelligence of the experts in charge of planning, estimates, the nation's accounts and all the organs created by the Fourth Republic, forget to note when their recommendations come off and when they fall through? It is not merely a question of determining if a measure is or is not effective, or even whom it helps and whom it harms. That the French state firmly intends to make the economic and financial machine work and that it has given proof to that effect we do not doubt, particularly since in this area, as in others, its braggadocio won't let you forget when it succeeds, just as its reticence doesn't let you suspect that it has failed. As we have said, prosperity is a general phenomenon in the West; France is not outstanding either for the level of its prosperity or for its rate of growth. On the other hand, France shows marked originality in the way in which its new affluence is distributed.

In fact, the principal subjects discussed in the economic and financial press during the last six years are the following:

1. Increasing divergence between the highest and lowest income brackets: or, if you prefer it stated another way, salaries in the average and lower income brackets have remained stationary. Only management salaries have kept pace with economic growth.

2. Increasing divergence between salaries in private enterprise and those in public service. The inadequacy of the latter has discouraged many people from entering public service, education suffering in particular.

3. Increasing divergence between salaried and nonsalaried incomes (bonuses, commissions, professional fees, expense accounts, clandestine usury, capital gains, particularly in real estate, which are not taxed).

[23] Heavy Franc; Balanced Budget; Gold.

4. Lack of a policy on incomes; that is, a policy that takes the real incomes into consideration, for all that the statisticians seem to know about are wages and salaries. No measures have been undertaken that would enable us to know the nature and extent of nonsalaried incomes, and thereby reveal what the true structure of the French economy is.

5. Increasingly unfair taxation, the inevitable result of the foregoing. The greater part of France's real wealth is unknown to the Treasury; and the state doesn't want the Treasury to know. What escapes taxation through this lacuna has to be made up by direct taxes on wages and other forms of income that cannot be hidden and by indirect taxes that fall on all sources of income without distinction.

6. The various measures which the Fifth Republic has taken to promote a sound financial structure and to stabilize prices have proved partially successful, but only at the expense of certain economic groups that used to be favored, while other groups continue to enjoy their privileges (and privileges they most certainly are, for the law, which should be common to all, is not applied to some).

7. Complete collapse of policy on public investments because of the expenses involved in producing the atomic bomb.

8. In the economic and financial sphere, as in all others, the public power strives to curb the dissemination of honest and accurate information and to publicize an inaccurate account of the national economy.

The people with whom you discuss any of these eight points fall into two groups: government officials, who privately hold opinions contrary to the ones that they express in public; and Leftists, who do the same. The latter, in their newspapers, force themselves to express reservations concerning the Fifth Republic's economic policy, but in private they cannot conceal their admiration for it. The financial and planning experts, who conceive, apply and publicly defend the Plan will tell you privately and with admirable frankness that any parts of the economic and financial policy that do not favor business or the *force de frappe* are mere eyewash and never come to anything.

And the Leftists, on the other hand, bedazzled by the bureaus, organization and programs, and remembering the aphorism that liberalism is old-fashioned, are enchanted by all this planning; a feeling of euphoria surges through them when the planners honor them from time to time with confidences at dinner, and they go into a state of ecstasy, like passengers who are shown the engine room on a ship. Besides, they are far from refusing to admit that the worker is happier now than he was in 1945, or the peasant happier now than in 1495, an improvement that in all fairness (for fairness is the hallmark of the Left) one must obviously credit to the Fifth Republic. Naturally, the really important thing, which is not only to find out whether the standard of living has risen, but whether it has risen as much as it possibly could have risen, and particularly whether it has risen for everyone in proportion to the overall increase in the national income, is not considered.

For Frenchmen, prosperity under the Fifth Republic is more a psychological state than a reality. It's their Moscow subway. When you have it drummed into you for years that you are the only people that owns its subway, you conclude *a fortiori* that what you own is the handsomest subway in the world. We who are so quick to laugh at the statistics of the Iron Curtain countries don't feel the least bit ridiculous when the President of the Republic, in his television and radio speech of December 31, 1964, tells us that in six years the budget estimates for education have increased 170 percent, when in reality they have increased . . . 14 percent.[24] The legend of prosperity has to be constantly fed by narcissistic

[24] "An optimistic but flattering balance sheet" by Gilbert Mathieu, *Le Monde,* January 2, 1965.

displays of self-satisfaction on the part of the government. But more serious still is the fact that economic documents and sources of information are falsified, and not just those that are destined for the mass public. The monthly studies of the National Institute of Statistics are, by order of the Minister of Finance, now shorn of all findings and conclusions, a measure taken because the Institute had had the audacity to affirm "that a stagnation in industrial production would probably start at the end of 1964 or the beginning of 1965"[25]—a prediction that was ill-mannered enough to come true. "Pressure from the Minister of Finance does not stop there: the disappearance of the *Weekly Bulletin of Statistics* has had the effect of suppressing, week after week, any recording of food prices, which showed increases more often than decreases."[26]

This falsification and suppression of facts extends to the very manner in which the budget is presented. Thus, in 1965 and contrary to official propaganda, government expenses increased at a faster rate than the gross national product; the amount set aside for civil expenses is, however, unchanged, while "the only investment category that will be speeded up next year is that for military equipment: +14.1 percent."[27] Finally, instead of being reduced, as promised, taxes were raised 16 percent.

The latter point is important, and I mention it again because everyone knows that France's attitude toward tax privileges has not changed since the time of the *Ancien Régime;* that is, France considers it normal for the nation to be divided into two categories: the larger and poorer, which pays a tax on its income; and the other, which is totally or partially exempt —legally then, *de facto* today.

The rate of *taxation* on incomes deriving from various

[25] *Le Monde,* January 9, 1965.
[26] *Le Monde,* January 9, 1965.
[27] "A Surprise Budget" by Gilbert Mathieu, *Le Monde,* November, 1964.

sources and ranging from the highest to the lowest rate is as follows:

1. Intellectual labor.
2. Manual labor.
3. Industrial and commercial bonuses; dividends; income from real estate. Professional fees.
4. Untaxed: capital.

It is clear, then, that the two things that are held in the greatest contempt in France are intellect and labor.

The sharply graduated income tax scale, intended to make up in some small way for tax evasion in the third category, becomes murderous for the intellectual as soon as his salary surpasses that of a manual laborer. A professor who has just won a teaching position by passing his *agrégé* examination earns about as much as a skilled laborer, while a professor who is not an *agrégé* earns about as much as an unskilled laborer. But as soon as the profits of intellectual labors reach a level that could be considered very modest by the third group's standards, say 2,500 francs a month [$500], as in the case of top-level technicians, engineers, *agrégés* with both seniority and overtime, writers and journalists—their tax becomes proportionately five to ten times greater than that of the third category. As for the professions, they take full advantage of the infinite possibilities for fraud that are open to them, and in this they enjoy a toleration that derives from the fact that, although these professions involve intelligence and specialized knowledge, they find their place in society through an act that is essentially commercial, not unlike retail merchandising. What the French scorn is the very concept of salary, salaried work to start with and intellectual salaried work above all else. Thus Georges Darien's prediction has come true: "Income tax, which you are hearing so much about and which will surely be upon us one day or another, is supposed to be a reform; the poor devils will see what it will cost them. They will come to realize, with an astonishment perhaps tinged with bitterness, that the income tax will be a real burden only on those who have no income."[28]

And so, in order to maintain the organic fiscal injustice, the main thing is to keep the people from finding out exactly what French incomes are and how they are distributed. Back in 1963 *Le Monde* wrote that "the policy on income, at once decisive and equitable," was "the first victim of the stabilization plan."[29] This is understandable, considering that "the disparity of incomes in our country ranges from one to more than one thousand, counting only the *categories* at either extreme and not isolated individual cases."[30] "Clearly there will be no attempt in the near future to bring French incomes into line and lessen the instances of shocking inequality," said *Le Monde* two years later. "Quite the contrary: the stabilization plan has aggravated social injustice by making the categories whose income it is easiest for the State to check up on pay the price for financial reorganization."[31]

Let us recall that in August, 1961, on the basis of a study by the National Institute of Statistics, the Minister of Finance published for the first time a table showing the distribution of incomes in France. Although this document revealed great inequalities, it apparently did not show the full extent of these inequalities. Specifically, it seemed to underestimate the number of French families with incomes between 300,000 and 800,000 odd francs a month.[32] Why? Because these incomes, which derive from industry, business and the professions, do not show up on the income tax returns. But how is anyone to believe that less than one percent of Frenchmen earn over $600

[28] Georges Darien, *La Belle France*, 1901. Republished in 1965 by J.-J. Pauvert.
[29] September 8, 1963.
[30] *Le Monde*, September 13, 1962.
[31] "Woe to the Weak" by Gilbert Mathieu, September 6-7, 1964.
[32] Between, roughly, $7,000 and $20,000 a year, or between $600 and $1,600 a month.—*Translator's note.*

a month when every day you meet people in the most mid-
dling of middle-class circles for whom such a sum is a mere
nothing? You have only to frequent hotels, restaurants, ga-
rages, electrical appliance stores and the like to see how many
people there are who pay one hundred francs [$20] for lunch
or count out cash for a television set or a new car as casually as
they would pay for a pack of Gauloises. Perhaps what explains
in part the social and political immobility of present-day
France is the advent of the "fairly rich," this new economic
class which is comfortably ensconced somewhere between the
old petty bourgeoisie and real wealth. For if the privileged
classes were as small as those in pre-Revolutionary France or
Czarist Russia, they could not, in view of the poverty or desti-
tution of the vast mass of workers, farmers, white collar
workers and civil servants, have held out so resolutely against
demands for reform. But, thanks to their relatively large numbers, they can cover up the fact that they are nonetheless a
minority; they melt into a mass instead of standing out, and
serve as a screen instead of as a target, spreading the myth of a
general prosperity, for you see them everywhere every day.
This is a good example of capitalist prosperity, pushing down
the social groups whose interests conflict and at the same time
covering up the conflict; for the prosperity of a rather large
minority permits the squandering of quite large sums of
money in conspicuous consumption.

By its very ostentation, prosperity seems to affect many
more consumers than it does in fact. Advertising constantly
creates new *desires*, which absorb all this easy money that
French capitalism is unable to channel into satisfying vital
necessities. To appease ten desires of five million people is not
the same as satisfying a single need of fifty million, but at a
distance it makes the same, if not a better impression. However, in order to conceal the fact that forty million human
beings are poor, you need to have at least five million privi-

leged people in the foreground—a figure which, representing as it does more than ten percent of the population, explains their strength and their ability to orientate the laws in their favor.

In the light of these statistics, it is evident that the traditional bourgeois and religious techniques for lulling and deceiving the populace have been highly effective. Indeed, how can one otherwise explain the fact that tens of millions of poverty-stricken Frenchmen, who are denied equality, whose basic rights of shelter, leisure, education and even breathing are trampled on, who are insulted not only by the way in which the greater part of the national revenue is wasted, but also by having taken from their salaries and wages the taxes that are used to subsidize the privileged interests who exploit them—how otherwise explain the fact that most of these tens of millions of Frenchmen in this relatively enlightened country nevertheless vote for conservative, authoritarian and clerical parties? Only ignorance and censorship could work this miracle, the only real economic miracle, and a lucrative one at that, wrought by the Fifth Republic. Thus, had a more detailed picture of French incomes been available, there is no telling what might have turned up.

Since the majority of Frenchmen on salary earned less than 500 francs a month [$100] in 1959[33] and less than 800 francs [$160] in 1963,[34] one may conclude that "the average increase in workers' *real* wages—after allowing for price increases—was thus less by half than the increase in industrial production, while the average increase in management salaries rose at the same rate." The salary range runs from 1 to 40. If we bear in mind that incomes range from 1 to over 1,000, we get some idea of where wage earners—even the highest-paid ones—rank on the income scale.

[33] *Le Monde,* November 29, 1959.
[34] *Le Monde,* November 24, 1963. As Gilbert Mathieu says, "Two-thirds of salaried workers earn less than 800F a month." *Vide* also *Le Monde* of November 11, 1964.

It does not surprise one, then, that the economic and financial section of *Le Monde* of November 1, 1964, rejoiced at the prospect of seeing French incomes finally come under "the fire of the Economic Council" (to quote the headline in its "Weekly Bulletin"). But a few days later the bulletin carried a quite different headline—"About-face of the Economic Council"—and went on to recount bitterly how the Council had pitifully turned tail when finally confronted with the responsibility of having seriously to investigate French incomes.

France's economic growth, then, is only about average for a Western industrialized country; the manner in which the state power has shared out the fruits of this growth is reactionary. Why has the Left been so warm in praising the positive aspects of this tendency of the French economy, and so lukewarm, even reluctant, in analyzing its faults and hypocrisies? In this as in many other areas, with the excuse of avoiding "infantile Leftism," there has not been a single manifestation of opposition since 1958—industrial strikes, peasant protests, Student Union resistance, the demands of the civil servants, criticism of the *force de frappe*, denunciation of the lies in the news and in official statistics, protests against the scandalous changes in the Penal Code which have stripped the citizen of his remaining guarantees, struggles to combat indirect censorship of books and fining of publishers, or the fight for nonreligious schooling—in short, there has not been a single act undertaken to support freedom of thought, social justice, respect for the individual or political democracy; not a single declaration or movement in favor of equality, law and a genuine constitution; no anti-governmental action that most of the leaders of the Left have not instantly and tirelessly attacked as outrageous, old-fashioned and uselessly extremist and, under the pretext of making more effective, that they did not finally discourage. There has been no opposition in France for seven years, except for that of mutinous soldiers and rioters from North Africa—which means that the only things that exist are submission and illegality. The sole opposition to the Right—at least the sole feared opposition—came from Right extremists. To oppose the present regime is to cut oneself off from the social body, and the Left's whole attitude shows that it accepts this verdict. Since its Marxist past constrains it to attack the Power, the Left feels easy only when it is able to attack it without hurting it, and approve it without admitting it.

As far as the majority of Leftist intellectuals is concerned, the explanation is simple: they were Leftists, indeed violent Stalinists, for as long as anyone thought that a Socialist-Communist revolution could take place in France, or more probably in France and Italy simultaneously. During this period, to be in the opposition meant one was taking one's place in the power structure of tomorrow. As soon as it became apparent that there would be no revolution in France—after the economic boom of 1952-1956, the crushing of the Hungarian uprising, which emphasized the isolation of the Communists, the bourgeoisification of the consumers, the helplessness of the various Leftist groups before the crimes of decolonialization, and, finally, the collapse of parliamentary democracy—many intellectuals of the Left began to realize that the sort of vaguely paternalistic dictatorship that had just taken power would be around for a long time to come. Then they aimed at brilliantly laying bare its merits, in accordance with a dialectic that I have frequently described in these pages, and only with great reluctance could they bring themselves to admit its shortcomings, when they didn't deny them categorically.

This intellectual and bourgeois Left feels perfectly at home in our monarchic society; it loves being close to the Power, hobnobbing with its members and retainers; humanly, it feels at ease with the representatives of moneyed interests, whom it admires and whose way of life and bad taste it strives to imitate. The Left agrees with the standards of success represented by titles, offices and diplomas, by official positions, by the influence of special-interest cliques made up of families or friends, by might itself—which takes the place of talent in its eyes; and it manages to criticize the political and religious Power only with such understanding and propriety that none of the careers that this Power can offer its elite is closed to the Left. In short, it seems that it was only the great fear of Fascism, which followed the Liberation and ended about 1955, that caused the studious youth of the French middle class to join the ranks of the Marxist Left. But, now that they have reached maturity, these scions of the bourgeoisie have found their real milieu, that of a paternalistic technocracy, of elite groups managing the people, of a government that tolerates gentle criticism from its well-heeled VIP's, who are free to poke innocent fun at chauvinistic pretensions to a grandeur that is designed to dupe only the naïve masses. In sum, it seems that the only way that the evolution of the Left, and particularly of the intellectual Left, in the last twenty years can be correctly interpreted, the only way that it falls into some sort of intelligible perspective, is to consider it in the light of a single structural and operational principle: opportunism.

It will, then, be thanks neither to its intellectual leaders, who for twenty years have been principally engaged in inventing excuses for the ruling power, nor to its people, reduced to ignorance by the censorship of political information, and to indolence by the novel pleasure of partial affluence, that the French will once again find the energy to govern themselves under a constitution that they have personally drawn up and approved, thus rejoining the great Western tradition of the Reign of Law. Decolonization interrupted this tradition, and caused the thread to be lost; but at the same time it showed that this tradition had never been really understood by the French, for whom the only enduring image of power is authoritarian and personal power.

To take part in politics or to be interested in politics means that one is able to relate one's desires and discontentments, one's needs and satisfactions, one's work, leisure, income, education, family, health, dignity, food and shelter to an act by which one joins in giving or refusing to give Power to a man or a group of men. It means being familiar with the legal measures which we are, or ought to be, able to take in order to influence these men in the way they use this power. Whence we conclude that "depoliticalization" in itself is an anomaly, so long as a state exists somewhere; depoliticalization should never be put forward as the inevitable consequence of the increasing complexity and specialization of modern problems. On the contrary, this complexity and specialization should cause a highly developed "politicalization," except where the people has been browbeaten. To write that one or another group of citizens is interested only in problems which concern its profession and not in politics, is interested in city planning and not in politics, in its standard of living and not in politics, in education and not in politics, in trade unions and not in politics, in commerce and not in politics, in short, in "concrete realities" and not in politics, to write this and to admit it, is to write and admit that an animal organism can function without a nervous system, under the pretext that an animal strives to eat, sleep, breathe and reproduce and not expressly to make his nervous system function. But in organisms the nervous system functions of its own accord, while in societies politics is like a nervous system that is created and maintained by the members thereof.

Politics has no more *raison d'être* than a nervous system if one considers it in isolation: but isolating it or isolating everything else in relation to it is precisely what "depoliticalization" is. As modern societies grow more and more complicated and technical, political sense should become all the more widespread and sophisticated; as their activities multiply, the connections between these activities and politics (that key synthesizing formula) should also multiply, change and become ever more clearly defined. To imagine the contrary, to proclaim, as does the Left, that the public today is interested in problems of "structure," organization, management and technique divorced from politics, is as futile as to believe that you can see with a glass eye. Of course, those in power are quite happy for the citizens to believe it, since the misleaders of the people have always dreamed, not of doing away with politics, but of being the only ones to engage in it.

With this aim in view, the first concern of oligarchs is to create institutions in such a way that their political personnel cannot be renewed. Democracy is a continuous mixing process, where new elements constantly emerge from the mass. In a modern dictatorship, on the other hand, the door must be shut, so that no man who rises out of the crowd can possibly establish contact with the political machinery, whose operators are in fact chosen by cooptation. And then they ask you: "Who could replace Mr. So and So? Whom do you propose? Show me a man who can do the job." Which, of course, can't be done: all the new men are outside and have no chance of making themselves heard, since the only way one can hope to rise out of anonymity is by supporting a program that citizens who are of age will vote for—not by pitting an unknown or vaguely familiar name against a well-known name. A country in which the citizens vote only for names, knowing nothing of the programs which these names represent, no longer deserves to be called a democracy. But this is unfortunate only if the country feels that it must be a democracy and suffers because it is not. In the opposite case—and France *is* the opposite case —one should cheer up and not try to make people realize that they are badly off when they don't realize it themselves. For more than two centuries, France has sought to find happiness and stability under regimes in which the people govern themselves through the intermediary of representatives whom they elect to carry out an established program which is known to all. It has never succeeded. One can only conclude, then, that France is not made for regimes of this sort. The glory of our generation will be that it plucked out this truth and established our true nature; and the glory of our intellectuals will be that, after centuries of ill-humor, they finally became reconciled with the nation.

SUMMARY

In France, the people as a whole take little or no part in
the cultural heritage of French civilization. The bad taste,
ignorance and ugly living quarters are especially striking in a
country which prides itself on the opposite. The true calling
of the French is not the intellectual but the military life. In
France, the military ideal is the prototype for all human ideals.
The Frenchman's concept of political power apes the military
principle. A misinterpretation of history gave rise to the image
of the French as the people of liberty and revolutions, even
though their whole nature inclines them in the opposite direction. They have constantly shown their contempt for
democratic regimes and democratic political figures, and their
voluntary submission to authority explains why all regimes
based on personal power quickly achieve a lasting success that
only catastrophes can upset. The French don't need to be
denied their freedom, particularly that of expression, for them
not to avail themselves of it. They have created the modern
dictatorship, adapted to an under-informed, affluent society.

Confronted with this new phenomenon, the French Left,
in its heart of hearts, has rallied to the authoritarian regime.
Analysis of various phenomena demonstrates its changed attitude: the end of the Algerian War, the Manifesto of the 121,
police repressions of student demonstrations, the status of
news and opinion, television, the Fifth Republic's economic
and cultural policies, "depoliticalization." A secret admiration

for the modern dictatorship has caused the Left to hold all serious attacks on it in abeyance. Leftist journalism specializes in equivocal editorials dedicated to so-called objective analysis, incomprehensible except when it comes to acknowledging the merits of personal power. The two Lefts. In eight years, the only effective opposition to the Right has come from the Extreme Right. For seven years, the Left has thwarted all criticism of personal power with this dodge: "That means you really support the Fourth Republic!" The birth of a class of so-called Leftist intellectuals, Marxists in 1948 and sheepish Gaullists today, who are overawed by positions, titles, and material and financial success and who pant after government careers. They belong to the same species as the lackeys of modern dictatorship.

Conclusion: it is not correct that the evolution of industrial, technical and affluent societies must perforce engender political apathy. In fact, it should be the other way round: increasing complexity should generate a heightened political sense. France, therefore, constitutes an exception, but it is happy this way, for it realizes itself most fully when it knows nothing of what its rulers are doing or what they intend doing. Thus: historic reconciliation of the French intellectuals with the nation in this new perspective.

Postscript

AFTER THE GENERAL'S RE-ELECTION

If, as I have said in the foregoing pages, the French are not fundamentally a democratic people, what conclusions can be drawn from the December 1965 presidential elections?

The results of the first ballot—which hardly anyone expected—showed the powerful effect of free access to information on a people who had been anesthetized by seven years of official propaganda. Nine-tenths of the voters do not read the newspapers, whose chief aim is to disseminate political and financial news; their only contact with the political world is television which, in France, together with the radio, is under state control. De Gaulle, therefore, runs no great risk by respecting, to a degree, the freedom of the press; moreover, to avoid problems, the press has grown accustomed to censoring itself.

Since the fundamental principle of the Gaullist regime is to govern in an authoritarian manner, yet never—or rarely—to cross the frontier that leads to real dictatorship, de Gaulle could not refuse the opposition candidates access to television during the campaign, however limited it might be by a special commission of control. For France this was incredible, an unheard of experience; for the first time the Fifth Republic was discussed before the majority of the people no longer in terms of a permanent miracle, but as one government existing among other possible governments, with its economic and diplomatic failures, its reactionary position on school and housing problems, and so on. The shock was tremendous. For this we should be thankful, especially since the opposition candidates managed to avoid all demagogy and proved what I assert in this book: objective reporting of news is the bread of modern democracy, and this alone can make an election significant in democratic terms.

Unfortunately, a total of one month of objective reporting and free discussion in seven years is not very much. Between the first and second ballots, the opposition candidate promised, should he win, to permit the Gaullists to appear regularly on television. De Gaulle, on the other hand, made no such promise.

Has France, despite Gaullism's spectacular failure on the first ballot, really changed in relation to the portrait which I have drawn in this book? I do not believe so. Even though de Gaulle did change the style of his campaign in the two weeks between the first ballot and the run-off, by speaking to the people in a more familiar, less disdainful manner, he has not in the least altered the basic tenets of his political philosophy. For him, it is impossible for several political factions to coexist in one country; if you are not a Gaullist, you are not a Frenchman. During the course of his campaign, he never proposed any concrete program to the citizens, nor did he ask them to understand the problems of France and the world; he simply pointed out that in their hearts the people knew he was right. He reasserted the doctrine of an authoritarian state in which opposition and disagreement is not a privilege, but a symptom of disease and betrayal. In spite of this he obtained 55% of the vote; the irrational respect for haughty authority had triumphed once again over the supposed French taste for lucid explanation. Hence I must continue to believe that the cure for our patient, France, her transformation into an adult country—a responsible democracy, mistress of her fate, and disdaining all mystical notions of the State—will still take a long time to achieve.

I must add that my book should not be taken as dealing exclusively with France, which serves only as an example. The same problem is shared by all so-called consumer, or "affluent," societies, in which one may observe the phenomenon described as depoliticalization. But if, for the first time in history, we have witnessed the birth or consolidation of societies in which it is possible for every citizen to satisfy his elementary needs, must we, contrary to the hopes of the philosophers of the past, pay for this satisfaction with the sacrifice of our individual intelligence and liberty, and our collective responsibility and freedom? The future of our civilization depends on the answer to this question.

Jean-François Revel

Paris, December 20, 1965